Edward Robert Pearce Edgcumbe

Zephyrus

A Holiday in Brazil and on the River Plate

Edward Robert Pearce Edgcumbe

Zephyrus
A Holiday in Brazil and on the River Plate

ISBN/EAN: 9783337232269

Printed in Europe, USA, Canada, Australia, Japan

Cover: Foto ©Andreas Hilbeck / pixelio.de

More available books at **www.hansebooks.com**

ZEPHYRUS

A HOLIDAY IN
BRAZIL AND ON THE RIVER PLATE

WITH ILLUSTRATIONS BY

E. R. PEARCE EDGCUMBE

LL.D.

'TUM ZEPHYRI POSUERE : PREMIT PLACIDA ÆQUORA PONTUS'

Æneid

London
CHATTO & WINDUS, PICCADILLY
1887

PREFACE.

I DO not know that any apology is needed for publishing a new book about Brazil and the countries of the River Plate ; for these lands are little known except to those who travel thither for business purposes. If some should think that in these pages I have dwelt unduly upon the economic side of life, I must plead that by profession I am a banker, and that ' there is nothing like leather.'

E. R. P. E.

SOMERLEIGH, DORCHESTER:
September 1887.

CONTENTS.

ZEPHYRUS.

CHAPTER I.

OVER THE SEA.

WE were making the most of our five-o'clock
tea on a cheerless November afternoon, and
discussing our next summer's wanderings,
when the suggestion was thrown out, 'Make
a start in the spring, leave the east wind
behind, and set sail for the tropics.'

The idea was so tempting that we quickly
decided to act upon it, and forthwith set about
ordering overland trunks and all other need-
fuls for a lengthened voyage.

Our course once mapped out—to the Brazils
and the River Plate—we elected to take
passage by the Royal Mail Line, as their
steamers touch at most of the places we wished

B

to visit. Then came advice from numerous
friends, advice of the most conflicting kind.
'Dress as in England,' said one experienced
traveller ; 'Bring plenty of light summer
things, and don't be afraid of having too much
luggage,' said a second ; 'Wear fairly thick
clothes, and take as little as you can,' said a
third. We are now in *our* turn experienced
travellers, and if asked what advice we should
give, it would be, ' Take as little as you can ;
be provided with a few garments adapted for
excessive heat, and do not omit a small store
of provisions, compressed tea, cocoa, tinned
milk, biscuits, an etna, and an india-rubber
hot bottle.'

We left England in the middle of February
with frost and snow on the ground. Twenty-
four hours later we were running peace-
fully across the Bay of Biscay, which was
on its good behaviour, and the day following
the temperature had so far changed that it
was quite pleasant to wash in cold water. On
the third morning out we were at Lisbon.

Lisbon lies stretching along the river-side

flanked with high hills towards the north and
facing, the busy open river and the hilly
country southwards, a charming situation.
The city itself is a horrible one for getting
about in, owing to the tremendous hills.
Nothing ever seems to have been done to modify
the gradients. It is like walking up and down

LISBON.

the sides of a house. The vehicles are
splendidly horsed, which is, indeed, a matter
of necessity and not of choice, and the horses
trot up the hills in a way that would make an
English horse stare. The houses are built in
expectation of another earthquake, the frame-

work being of wood and the outsides only cased with stone or brick. The shops contain little to tempt one. We went to the opera in the evening—the singing was good, but the performers were all dressed like inferior rag dolls and the scenery was to match.

In a neglected grave in the English burial-ground lies the greatest of novelists, Henry

LISBON, LOOKING OUT TO SEA.

Fielding. Hither he came in the spring, and here he died in the fall, of 1754. Here it was that he penned the last of his writings, brimful of humour, the ' Voyage to Lisbon.'

On the river I took note of a trim well-built steamer, and, on inquiring her calling, found she was exclusively employed carrying wine from Lisbon to Bordeaux, to be there diluted into claret for the English market. We left Lisbon on Saturday evening, looking for an easy run of ten days to Pernambuco. Next morning when we turned out it was just a bit rolly. Presently we heard a tremendous crash of crockery, and, looking out of the cabin, I found that the ship had given a lurch which had sent the whole of the breakfast flying. The fiddles were put on the tables, and breakfast relaid, but very few made an appearance. I retired rather promptly after a very frugal repast to my cabin. While sitting on my bunk, feeling somewhat disconsolate, I heard a rush of falling water and a scurrying to and fro ; then after a short space another rush of water and a great turmoil without ; but I was not in an investigating frame of mind, so was inclined to let it pass. Then a sailor put his head in at my cabin door, and inquired, 'Any water in this cabin ? ' ' No,' said I, rather tartly, yet with a subdued sense of having something to be thankful for after all. But

my sense of satisfaction was to be soon dis-
pelled; for presently a streak of dirty water
ran like a snake across my cabin ; then more
and more as the vessel rolled and pitched,
leaping and dancing with boisterous delight.
Six inches of water on a stationary floor is one
thing ; but six inches in a cabin which is
tilted at every angle in thirty seconds is another. It rushed hither and thither, splashed,
gurgled, and hissed. It carried off boots,
slippers, and socks, got into our boxes, saturated our biscuits, wetted the bedding, and in
two minutes turned the whole place into a
reeking, chilly, wave-swept cavern. I rushed
about, trying to save what I could, and then,
hearing loud voices without, I inquired of the
chief officer, ' Where does the water come
from? ' ' I can't say,' was the answer. This
is a cheerful state of things, thought I, when
crash came tons of water down the fore-hatch-
way, which had not been battened down, and
the mystery was explained. For the next
half-hour they were battening down the
hatchway, and swabbing up, but our cabin

was perfectly uninhabitable for the rest of the day ; so I sought refuge, accompanied by a hot bottle, in the upper saloon. We ran all day under steam and canvas, with the wind athwart the beam. About seven o'clock in the evening the wind suddenly went down, and, as the wind dropped, the vessel, being no longer keeled over by her sails, righted. Just then we had the ill-luck to be struck by a very heavy sea, which swept one of the life-boats clean away, in which were stored all our fresh vegetables for the next ten days' con-sumption. Away, too, went the pigs, their house and all. One more vast mass of water came trampling over the deck, and then the storm was over.

At daybreak on the third day after leaving Lisbon, we passed the Peak of Teneriffe, standing like a gaunt sentinel wrapped in the early morning mists. A few hours later we sighted several more of the Canary Isles. This was the last we saw of what geographers call the Eastern Hemisphere. Two days later we were in the tropics. The sea-water in the baths

was now quite hot, and the Portuguese men of
war (Nautilus) appeared sailing about in prodigious numbers. Clearly this the place to

> Learn of the little Nautilus to sail,
> Spread the thin oar and catch the driving gale.

In the languid swooning air of the Doldrums, we soon became quite child-like—
amused by the merest trifles—veritable lotus
eaters in mind and body. Yet delightful
dreamy days were these, lying in the open

FERNANDO NORONHA.

gun-ports, shaded from the sun, with the
breezes playing over the smiling many-dimpled
waste of waters—days not soon to be forgotten.
Every port was now kept wide open day and
night, and every breath of air was welcomed.
At night as I lay awake in my berth by the
open port, I could hear in answer to the ship's

bell ringing out the hours, the musical voice of the watch faintly echoing back from aloft through the still night air, ' All's well.' A cheery and soothing sound.

The first land we sighted of the new world was Fernando Noronha with its rugged peaks ; the home of murderers, for hither are sent the cut-throats of Brazil, the Emperor (Dom Pedro II.) having virtually abolished capital punishment by the simple expedient of refusing to sign the warrants of execution ; this branch of the executive not being dele-gated to a minister as in England.

•

CHAPTER II.

THE TROPICS.

On the tenth day out from Lisbon we arrived at Pernambuco. The city lies as flat as Venice on the water, simmering up all white and hot just between sea and sky, while

PERNAMBUCO.

stretching far away on either hand along the coast, stand forests of stately slender palms, throwing up their thousand sprays of verdure to the blue heaven. We went ashore and saw the narrow, crowded, picturesque old town,

the market and the long outlying streets
of modern houses, capacious but unbeautiful.
We trammed in all directions over the city by
the 'bond' as it is called, and amongst other
things came across a new beast of burden, to
wit, a sheep, harnessed in a little cart, going
round with the dusky baker at a brisk trot

NATURAL BREAKWATER, PERNAMBUCO.

from house to house, and doing its work to
all appearance most efficiently.

Pernambuco owes its importance as a seaport to a long straight reef of rock, which
forms a natural breakwater and secures the
city a splendid harbour. Outside this reef a
heavy sea is always running, due to two tides
meeting. This makes going ashore from a ship

moored in the offing a perilous matter even
on a calm day. The difficulties of it have
developed in the boatmen a remarkable cat-
like nimbleness of hand and foot. The fishermen of this coast go to sea on little rafts

JANGUARDAS.

called janguardas, consisting of four or five
logs braced together, propelled by a triangular
snow-white sail poised endways. At a distance these little craft look like mere white
pinions, the log deck being entirely hidden by
the water.

As the sea sweeps over them perpetually, the janguarda sailor is always wet to the knees, but as the water is quite warm from the heat of the sun, the fishermen do not regard this as an inconvenience. We passed janguardas quite sixty miles from shore. They are very stable, but liable to sink after being thirty-six hours at sea, from the wood absorbing too much water. As there is always some risk of being washed overboard, janguardas are provided with hempen loops to stay oneself by.

An immersion to the oily negro is merely a discomfort, but to the white man a danger ; for the dainty sharks which abound in these waters, though they will hardly look at a black man, devour a white man with avidity. Some of the janguardas, as in the sketch, have a little raised platform thatched over for shelter and rest at night.

The coloured people of Pernambuco appear to be both healthy and vigorous, but the pure whites seemed as if they drooped under the scorching blaze of the tropic sun ; many of them looking as if visibly touched by the finger of death. To the effect of the climate is probably due, in a large degree, the many cripples and deformities in human shape we could not avoid noticing. Perhaps the most delightful part of Pernambuco is the plaza at the quay, where one can sit under magnolias as big as forest trees, and gaze by the hour together out upon the blue sea.

After the loss of our fruit and vegetables in the storm, we were especially glad of the fresh supply we procured at Pernambuco. Pine-apples, although late in the season, were delicious, and most refreshing—tender, juicy, and glorious in colour ; so different from Covent Garden pine-apples. Wreaths of bananas of exquisitely delicate flavour. The correct thing is to eat them with large slices of Dutch cheese ; a taste which I think is due to cultivation, as it does not appear to be innate. Loquats, a small, round, dark yellow fruit, about the size of a Tangerine orange, with a large stone in the centre ; in fact, it seems chiefly skin and stone ; but for all that greatly appreciated by the Brazilians. The loquat when in blossom is a pretty little tree covered with sweet scented spikes of creamy white flowers. Oranges—called 'Bahia oranges' —such juicy fellows, melting in the mouth.

HUT WITH BANANA PALMS NEAR MACEIO.

Our next place of call was Maceio (Măc-c̄-ō). We landed and took the 'bond' southwards for about two miles out of the town, through the most glorious tropical vegetation dotted with the untidy, unkempt colour-washed stucco dwellings of the blacks or semi-blacks, who sat about the doors of their houses wholly absorbed in the serious contemplation of nothing—while their dusky progeny played in the roadway very simply clad in their birthday suits. At the terminus of the 'bond' we fell in with some lace-makers and made some satisfactory purchases. On our way back to Maceio we came upon a funeral just making ready to start, and found that people were even buried by means of the 'bond,'

THE HEARSE.

the hearse in this case being a railway truck elaborately resplendent in gold and silver tinsel on a black-velvet draping, and having in the centre, to carry the coffin, a sort of raised altar, similarly decorated.

Our next place of call was Bahia, grandly situated, as all the old Jesuit cities are, on a long low bluff, looking across the wide placid harbour to the deep blue distant mountains.

The best part of the town is built along upon the high ground some 200 feet above the sea. The abrupt hill-side is draped with bananas and the cocoa-palm, and below on the sea-level is the lower town where the colossal Bahia negroes, redolent of oil, bask in the sun. The arms of some of the women are bigger than many an English waist. The teeth and lips are monstrous, and their tattooed cheeks add to their extraordinary charms. The most typical negroes are jet black, and repulsively ugly, but they are of every shade and colour from black up to a dingy brown. One, strange to say, had carrotty hair and a complexion to suit, yet retained in matted hair and form of lips and jowl every point of the pure negro.

We ascended to the upper town by the lift of which I have a vivid recollection, the machinery being lubricated with castor oil, the cheapest oil here. From the Plaza to which the lift rises, there is a splendid view of the sweeping bay and distant mountains, the shipping lying immediately below in the foreground. The Plaza itself is a true bit of

antiquity, with a church and municipal buildings of a character that would not be out of
place in an old Italian city. From here we
took the 'bond' to Victoria, a charming off-
shoot of the city nestling on the Atlantic
shore. On the way thither we alighted at
what looked like a promising place for breakfast
and were not disappointed. We were taken to
a long room, if room it can be called; for,
though it was covered in overhead, the sides
were open, save for a deep skirting banked in
on either side by green bananas, tree ferns,
and bright flowers. A negro in spotless white
cotton attire, glittering with diamonds, moved
noiselessly about on bare feet, and laid before
us a capital breakfast with good bread, fresh
butter, and sweet milk. A delightful repast
enough to those who have been at sea for
days knowing nothing but tinned milk and
salt butter and ship bread.

Navigation in the neighbourhood of Bahia
is especially difficult owing to numerous reefs
and rocks, and from Pernambuco to the River
Plate generally is not unattended with risk,

as rocks and shoals are numerous, and the sea is indifferently charted. On her very next voyage out, the steamer we were on board struck on a rock. The Brazilian Empire and the River Plate republics practically refuse to chart their own coasts, on the plea that as they have no mercantile navy they are not concerned to do it.

The result is that mariners still steer by

BAHIA LIGHTHOUSE.

the chart made by Captain Fitzroy (with whom sailed Darwin in the 'Beagle') more than fifty years ago, corrected and amended from time to time by the costly process of reported wrecks on uncharted rocks and shoals. As storms are infrequent, there is little danger of loss of life, even if a vessel founders. But the loss of all one's baggage

may easily arise from shipwreck, and in a land
where money will not replace one's goods save
in a style unpalatable to an Englishman, such
a catastrophe may well be no slight inconvenience. Some of our numerous gun-boats might
be usefully employed in recharting these seas.

Boats come off at Bahia—and also at
Maceio and Pernambuco — to
homeward-bound ships, with
marmosets, parrots, monkeys,
cardinal birds, raccoons, and
other beasties for sale. A brisk
traffic is done in green parrots
at about three to five shillings
each, and in marmoset monkeys
at one shilling apiece. We
were rather drawn towards the
little marmoset monkeys, but
would not buy one, as we hardly
thought it fair to transport them
to a climate where their exist-

LITTLE 'WAIF.'

ence, as long as it drags on,
must be more or less miserable. In spite
of our good resolutions, however, we became

possessed of one ; for after the boats had left, and we were on our way once more, I found, running at large in the rigging, un-claimed, one of the prettiest little marmosets. We took charge of him and furnished him with a comfortable home in our cabin—a chattering little mortal, equally fond of a fresh grape and a blue-bottle fly. Little 'Waif,' as we called him, lived happily enough through the summer, but when the November days came round, he became peevish and husky, and at last one evening went to sleep and woke no more.

.

CHAPTER III.

RIO TO TIJUCA.

WE reached Rio on the nineteenth morning
after leaving England. It is impossible for
me to picture in words the beauty of the approach to Rio as we steamed in at daybreak
through the narrow gateway in the mountains,
flushing first deep purple, then crimson and
rose-colour, in the streams of light which ascended from the east, harbingers of the full
blaze of the tropical sun. Although the entrance to the Bay of Rio is a mile wide, its true
width is so dwarfed by the lofty mountains
that stand on either side that it looks like a mere
gap. Once within the gateway in the hills, the
mighty harbour stretches out into a grand
lake thirty miles across, completely girdled
round by mountain ranges. Sydney and the

Golden Horn are the only two places which are ever compared with Rio in respect of beauty. With Sydney I am not acquainted, so cannot judge ; but of Constantinople I can unhesitatingly say that it will not bear comparison with Rio. The name of Rio (river) is a misnomer. The Jesuit discoverers en-

BAY OF THE RIO FROM ORGAN MOUNTAINS.

tered the bay on St. John's day, and, thinking it to be the mouth of a river, they called it Rio de Janeiro.

We learned upon arrival that yellow-fever was bad in the city, and being told that it was especially likely to attack new comers, we deemed it prudent not to remain in Rio, so determined to go to Tijuca. We walked

through Rio, which looked both gay and busy ;
all the shops being open, and owing to its being
Sunday all the people wearing their brightest
apparel. The streets are very picturesque,
with a strong old Spanish flavour about their
appearance ; the shops excellent, displaying
wares of every kind, high in quality and high
in price. The market-place was full of life
and bustle, with all its strange colouring of
dark humanity in brilliant costumes, luscious
fruits, gaudy parrots and other birds—most
delectable to the artistic eye. Peculiar to Rio
are the flowers of various kinds made from
the feathers of birds, and I must admit,
though I do so with reluctance, that many of
these feather flowers are very beautiful. We
had a special 'bond' to take us onward, and
glorious was the scenery as we crept up the
mountain side to Tijuca, romantically perched
on a saddle between the Bay of Rio and the
Atlantic.

In spite of the great heat, the grass and
many of the trees were intensely green, no
doubt owing to the drenching morning dews.

All the way to Tijuca we were ascending,
and the woods on either side were aglow with
colour, purple and gold prevailing. The bare
rock cropping out in places showed the
scoring and polishing action of vast glaciers ;
and now where ice once lay in masses there
grow—all wild—palms of every kind, bananas
with enormous whorls of fruit, bread-fruit
and mango trees, poinsettias, various kinds
of azaleas, white and crimson mimosa, bushes
of plumbago, gigantic cacti, and innumerable
trees and flowers we knew not. Fine maidenhair fern growing everywhere, cropping out
in the stony roads, by the wayside, and
crowning the walls with a delicate green
fringe, greenhouse ferns growing in the most
luxuriant profusion, fairly exhausting every
term of admiration we were masters of. As
we crept up higher and higher we got the
most charming peeps of the bay below us and
the mountains round about. Away to the
right the Corco Vada, and at its foot the
botanical gardens famed for their stately
avenues of soaring palm trees which we

visited later. Before we quite reached the top
we quitted the 'bond' for a carriage drawn by
four mules. The crest once turned we were
rattled down at a headlong pace, banged round
corners anyhow, and bumped up and down
on our seats like india-rubber balls. This we

BAY OF RIO, WITH CORCO VADA AND PEAK OF TIJUCA
IN THE BACKGROUND.

found to be quite the usual style of driving,
yet accidents seldom happen unless a wheel
comes off, which they regard, however, as a
trifle. Only a few days after this, before our
nerves had quite come round to their ways, I
ventured to remonstrate with the driver for
descending a mountain road at what I thought

a break-neck pace without putting on the drag. He just glanced at me, and waving his hand with a gentle deprecatory air, merely remarked, ' The drag is out of order.'

We soon settled down in our comfortable rooms at White's Hotel ; palatial they seemed after our diminutive cabin. On the one side they opened right upon the courtyard with a fountain trickling under a bank of flowers. On the other side we stepped into a balcony, where we used to sit in our rocking chairs for hours together, looking out upon the mountain sides clothed with luxuriant vegetation. We usually rose at five o'clock. The morning light was then just fringing the mountains and the freshness was most exhilarating. The first thing was to journey to the bath, a running brook, leaping down amongst the rocks on the mountain side, waylaid and led into a grove of lofty bamboos. There in the midst is a large stone bath from every crack and crevice of which springs a wealth of maidenhair fern ; flowing out again, the water makes a descent of several feet, first

passing over a broad flat stone, underneath
which one can stand and get deliciously
drenched, while overhead the trellis-work is
laden with heavy clusters of the beautiful
bougainvillea. Just one of those romantic
bathing-places one is accustomed to see in
Claude's pictures—fit only for gods and classic
nymphs. After a leisurely bath, followed by
coffee and rolls, we rambled in the woods, returning by ten at latest. From ten o'clock
till four the heat kept us within doors, sketching flowers, reading and dozing, and then we
were out again till nearly seven, by which time
it was dark. Everything was so new and so
beautiful that the days seemed to fly by. To
a European it might be another planet, so utterly is nature in all her forms unlike what we
are accustomed to at home. Much of our time
was taken up in botanising. The flowers are
many of them so filmy in texture that we found
it impossible to dry them successfully in
presses. Some of them dropped to pieces so
quickly that it was difficult even to get them
home and rapidly sketch them before they died.

The flower of the mahogany tree is like a
creamy plume of feathers, but so filmy that
it drops almost as soon as plucked, and
many attempts were made before we succeeded
in getting one safely home. It is very curious
how nearly all the flowers are either brilliant

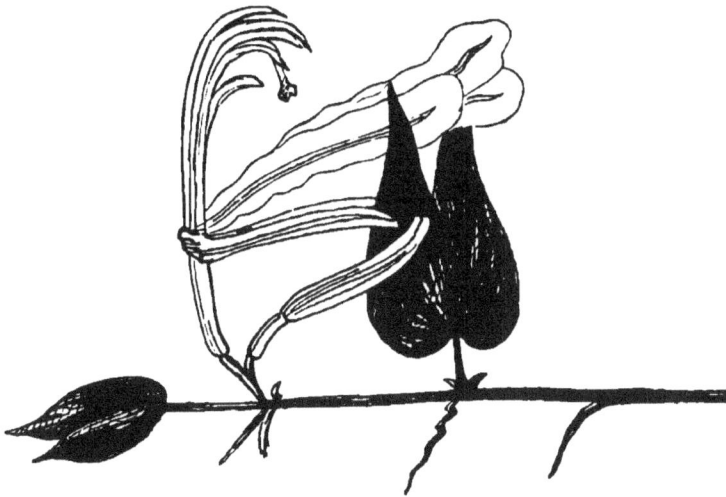

FLOWER OF MAHOGANY TREE.

crimson, yellow, or reddish purple; and
how every different walk seems to be furnished with a different set of flowers. Pale
flowers are rare. Of blue flowers we only
found one.

Sketching out of doors is well-nigh an

impossibility. The insects simply will not
allow it. If one makes an attempt to settle
down to sketch, several small forces of the
enemy at once begin the attack. As soon
as these have been beaten off, troops of others
appear and march and counter-march in the
most excruciatingly irritating way over the
lumps raised by the first comers. Others get
upon the paper, another lot gets into the paint
box, and yet another tribe drink up the paint
upon one's brush before one can get it on to
the paper. After several vain attempts I gave
up the struggle.

The lustrous tinted humming-birds are
the only birds that show themselves freely in
the sunlight (except vultures), darting from
flower to flower and hovering over them with
scarcely perceptible motion of the wing. The
other birds seem to fear the light and fly from
tree to tree hurriedly as if to escape the fierce
glare. But their shrill notes may be often
heard in the woods, and the chatter and sharp
squeak of the monkeys, and for ever and for
ever a kind of loud buzz of insects of all stations

and degrees. This buzzing never ceases,
always growing louder during the hottest
hours of the day. The noise that dominates
all, ever piercing the air most shrilly, is the
whirr of the cicada—a species of grasshopper.
They sit about in every tree, cicada answering
cicada,—beginning with a buzzing sound
which gets louder and louder as it rises up the
scale, and winding up with a piercing whistle.
It takes the cicada from 15 to 20 seconds to
ascend from a low buzzing sound to a shrill
whistle, and how so small an insect can make
such a tremendous noise—as loud almost as a
steam whistle—is a marvel. Just under our
balcony a little brook gurgled refreshingly :
by its side grew some crimson bignonia trees
about 12 feet high, clumps of bamboos 60
feet ·high, palms and tree ferns, and most
beautiful of all a large mimosa covered all over
with large rich, crimson, tufty blossoms,
circular balls of fine crimson hairs about 4
inches in diameter. The humming-birds were
especially fond of this mimosa, and were always
hovering over it, their lustrous green and

bronze colours showing off to advantage against the crimson blossoms. After dark the brook was alive with brilliant fire-flies, the great bats came sailing out and the owls began to screech, while above the mountain tops appeared the two constellations of the Cross, the Southern Cross, and the still more beautiful false Cross.

CHAPTER IV.

AN OLD FELON.

OUR abode at Tijuca was White's Hotel, a delightful rambling place with a curious history.
Some 40 years ago an old Frenchman took up
his residence here, and built for his home the
oldest part of what is now White's Hotel. He
lived a studiously retired life, never going
down to Rio, and from his unsociable nature
came to be regarded as a queer character by
the few neighbours round about. Rio was not
then so easily reached as now, there being only
rough mule tracks to the city. After living a
lonely life for some twelve years one of the old
Frenchman's slaves ran away. The slave was
captured in Rio, and word was sent to his
master that if he would come down and
identify the fugitive slave, he could have him

D

back. To Rio he went, and when there the
chief of the police recognised him as one who
had been ' wanted ' some twelve years before.
He was taken into custody and eventually sent
to Paris, there tried for forgery, convicted, and
transported to Algiers for life. His property at
Tijuca was sold for a song, and the purchaser,
finding the air invigorating, made it a sort of
sanatorium, and gradually it became changed
into a regular hotel.

The old Frenchman of Tijuca could not
have been aware of the proper method of stating
his case to the police, or he might have saved
himself his return journey to Paris, if what I
heard said of the ways of the Brazilian police is
to be trusted. If one may judge by more recent
events, it seems that they are a body not wholly
without guile. It was only the day before we
landed at Rio that it became generally known
there that the cashier of the English Bank of
Rio, a Brazilian, had absconded, and that there
was a deficiency in the notes he had in his
charge (the circulation is carried on entirely
in paper money) amounting to some 20,000*l.*

He had been living in a style beyond his visible
means, horse-racing, and generally plunging.
I inquired how he could escape from the
country. The reply was that he would not
do that, he would go into the interior. But
would he not then be easily taken, I asked.
' Oh no, not if he settled matters with the
police. That is easily done.'

My friend went on to say that he thought
the absconding cashier might ' safely return,
for no jury would convict him.' I thought
at the time that this was uttered sarcastically,
but, if so, it turned out to be only too true,
for I afterwards heard that the defaulting
cashier was tried by a Rio jury and actually
acquitted. The inability to be strictly honest
in times of temptation gives a great advantage
to Englishmen, who for all positions of trust
are held in high esteem. One day, when
changing a circular note at a branch of one
of the English banks, the cashier (a Brazilian)
gave me short change. After a protest he
handed me the full amount. Such a thing
would be unheard of, I imagine, in any bank

in England. The railway companies have to
maintain an elaborate system of checks to
prevent their employés from returning less
than the full amount taken by the companies,
yet even with these precautions I suspect that
a certain amount slips away. As showing
indirectly the want of honesty there is amongst
the people, fire insurance offices have to charge
higher premiums than they do in Europe, yet
the danger of fire in their houses, as compared
with ourselves at home, is infinitesimal; for
it never being cold enough to make a fire
necessary for warmth's sake, the only fire in
the house is a charcoal stove for cooking
purposes. So slight is the risk of fire in
private houses that it is said that 'there were
no fires in Rio before the insurance offices
came.' With regard to their infirmities in
the matter of truthfulness, a native put it to
me very neatly, though in somewhat broken
English, ' There is no place where they miss
more the truth.'

CHAPTER V.

'BICHOS.'

WE were the only *bonâ fide* travellers in the hotel at Tijuca. All the other occupants were merchants from Rio, with their wives and families, or well-paid clerks who seemed thoroughly to enjoy life — kindly friendly people, much accustomed to social ways, many of them living permanently, when in Rio, in large comfortable well-appointed boarding-houses.

After dusk the barata moves about with the activity of a gigantic black-beetle, which it closely resembles in form. It is an insect nearly as long and as broad as one's first finger, and of a dirty brown hue. It has an omnivorous appetite, with a special weakness for silk dresses, boots, kid gloves, and the leather bindings of books. The ants are

equally omnivorous, and their pertinacity nothing can balk. They always found out our
box of provisions, and do what we would there
was always a stream of them coming and
going to it, finding their way somehow even
into the tightly fitting tin cases inside it.
They are so dreadfully industrious that they
work all night. I found them just as busy at
two o'clock, three o'clock, and four o'clock in
the night, as during any other hours of the
twenty-four. It is owing to baratas and ants
that ancient documents are said to be things
unknown in the Brazils. A century at most
completes the span of life of records of all
descriptions. There is absolutely no chance
of unearthing some store of forgotten letters
or other papers from some newly discovered
hiding place, for the ' bichos ' will long ago
have digested them. Every member of the
animal and insect world in this country is called
a ' bicho.' Everything is a ' bicho ' (bee-co)
from a mosquito to an ostrich, the term being a
much more comprehensive one than the ' bug '
of the United States. The ordinary house-fly

of England, expanded under the favourable
conditions of tropical life almost to the dimen-
sions of a blue-bottle, stands quite in the first
rank of objectionable 'bichos.' His imper-
tinence and familiarity, combined with the
excessive number of his relations, always rendered every meal simply a physical struggle.
The spiders are, many of them, very beautiful,
and some of them simply gigantic. One day
I was walking along a narrow boulder-strewn
road towards the sea, and on looking up
almost said, 'What! telegraph wires down
this way!' but before the words had passed
my lips I looked again, and saw that they
were the telegraphic lines of a huge spider, a
fine striped beast sitting at the end waiting
for news.

The beetle family are numerous, and many
of them are very beautiful, their iridescent
coats of various metallic colours making them
gleam like gems. The king of the tribe, as to
size, is here sketched, but in colour he is unin-
teresting, being of a rusty black hue.

All kinds of strange bichos, attracted by

the lamp light, came in after dusk at our open
windows; one of them was the praying mantis
(μάντις — soothsayer), about which many
legends are current. It is supposed from its
praying attitude to act as a kind of guardian
angel which leads lost travellers home, but in

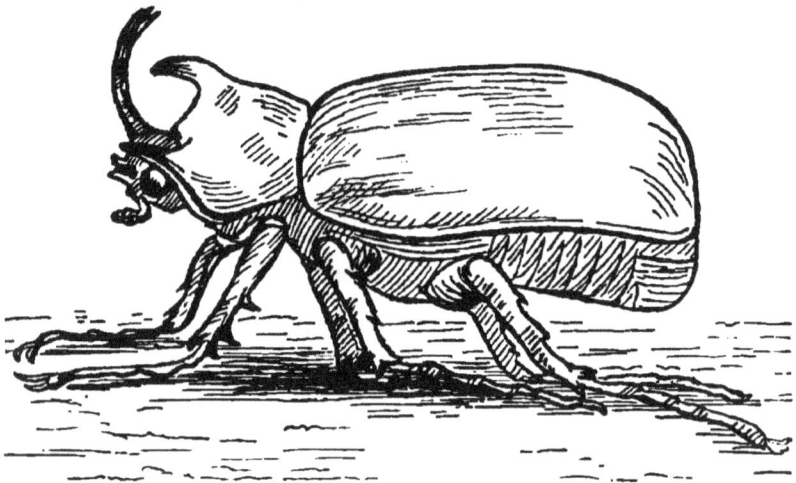

GREAT BRAZILIAN BEETLE (LIFE SIZE).

truth its ways are not saintly at all. Those
deceptive arms, clasped as if in prayer, are
powerful weapons of destruction, freely used for
the slaying of every sort and kind of the smaller
bichos, even frogs and lizards not escaping this
bloodthirsty little creature. The butterflies are
splendid fellows, all glorious in colour, sailing

about in the brightest sunlight and adding greatly to the beauty of the gay flowers they light on. Great azure-winged butterflies, eight inches from tip to tip, and many other sorts of giant size, their lovely plumage vying even with that of the humming birds, resplendent though their raiment is, as they glitter and glance in the sunlight.

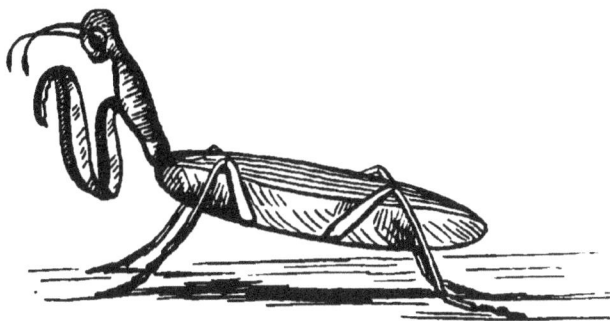

PRAYING MANTIS.

One has to be very careful in handling branches of trees and shrubs, as most of them are armed with large sharp thorns, while in others the bark grows in knife-like ridges which cut sharply into the flesh if grasped. At Tijuca we first came across the mango ; it is a fruit to be enjoyed in private, for it is juicy, and sticky, and runs about in an un-

seemly fashion. ' I like to eat mangoes in my
bath,' said an American friend to me; ' they
run about too much elsewhere.' We made an
excursion one day on ponies to the peak of
Tijuca, where we obtained a magnificent view
of the bay of Rio and the grand range of the
Organ Mountains. The way to the peak, all
but the last bit of it, wound up through the
woods. Beautiful creepers hung their tresses
in profusion from the trees. Orchids grew in
and out among the branches, but for the most
part out of reach. They affix themselves so
tenaciously that even a well-directed brick-bat
will not dislodge them. The only way to get
at them is to take a small black boy out with
one to climb the trees. On our way up, my
wife espied on a tree trunk what looked at
first sight like a mouse. She dismounted in
order to transfer it to her tin collecting box.
Immediately she took hold of it—luckily with
a gloved hand—she gave a slight scream; the
caterpillar—for caterpillar it was, and is here
drawn—sent a sharp shock of electricity, or
something like it, through her. Her hand was

painful for the rest of the day. We learnt afterwards that if this bicho is touched with the unprotected hand, both hand and arm swell up, causing much pain, sometimes accompanied for a day or two, by fever.

About two miles from Tijuca, on the side

CATERPILLAR (LIFE SIZE).

towards the Atlantic, and well worthy of a visit, are several boulders of enormous size piled one upon another. Some of them are so poised that they afford a sort of shelter, and from this the place is known by the name of the caverns. The largest boulder covers a space sixty feet long by forty-five feet wide, tilted just high enough to admit of one's walking underneath. It has been much disputed as to whether these boulders are erratic boulders transported by ice action, or whether they may be accounted for by water channels only. They are composed of a soft granite, and in any colder country would long centuries ago have been destroyed by the forces of frost and ice.

CHAPTER VI.

THE BRAZILIAN.

FROM Tijuca we went down to Rio, crossed
the bay nine miles by steamer, and crept up
the steep mountain-side by rail to Petropolis,
getting glorious views of the bay of Rio, with
the surrounding mountains, as we ascended.
Petropolis is a fashionable watering-place,
with smart houses and well-kept roads ; the
population is remarkably free from duskiness,
and generally prides itself upon its European
aspect. The Emperor has a country palace
here, in which he resides during most of the
summer. He has much endeared himself to
his people by his simple mode of life and unos-
tentatious, unceremonious, democratic ways.

In Brazil one is expected to know everything intuitively. Inquiries are of no avail.

At the best hotel at Petropolis they had no
time-tables of the trains. They did not know
when the diligence started, or anything we
wanted to know. They did not even know

CASCATINA, NEAR PETROPOLIS.

the cost of a telegram to Rio, and seemed
quite surprised at the inquiry being made.
At the post-office they were out of post-cards
and foreign stamps. The post-box for the
whole town was not much bigger than a tea-

caddy, and when a letter was dropped in, the post-master came out as if to survey the person who could be so strange as to write one. The middle-class Brazilian was in great force at Petropolis. He seems to be a most illiterate person. Book shops are almost unknown, newspapers even are rare, and as poor as they are rare. On two occasions only did I see Brazilians reading books ; one was a professor at Pernambuco University, the other was a student preparing for an examination.

The Brazilian father and mother live with their children always about them, and spoil them to the utmost. A Brazilian child is worse than a mosquito on the war path. Brazilian houses have no nurseries, and, as it is considered cruel to put the poor little dears to bed during the day, one has the pleasure of their company without any intermission. One may be coming down stairs in a hurry and find the landing blocked by an admiring group, much too absorbed to let one pass, gathered round some little bellowing parcel dressed like an exhibition doll. The dining-

room is generally the favourite resort of these
favoured little mortals, and their hunting-
ground, par excellence ; there, when not employed in devouring whatever they can get
hold of, they run races round the table and
criticise the ' Inglesi.' There were four children in one family ranging in age from eighteen months to seven years. These all dined
with their parents at seven o'clock. There
were two attendants to look after these children—a very exceptional thing—whose attention was entirely concentrated at the commencement of each meal upon the baby, who
always objected with much screaming and
gurgling to having soup poured down its
throat; the soup once safely disposed of by
means of some good slaps on the back, this
youngster partook of a few odds and ends and
was carried out. Then attention was given to
the next two, whose mouths were just on a
level with the table. These plied their knives
and fists with a skill which was clearly inherent. It was an unlovely sight, but one
could not help gazing and wondering what

would happen next. During the interval between the courses the two, aged four and six years old, took runs round the room as long as they were able, then gradually succumbed and were in turn carried out in a comatose state on the nurse's shoulders. The eldest struggled manfully to the end, never missing anything till he too was *hors de combat*. After dinner they quickly revived, ran riot in the balconies, took the most comfortable rocking chairs, and banged out with the most irritating iteration one bar of music on the piano. They certainly were *enfants terribles*, but children in the English sense do not exist in Brazil. The smallest girls had bangles and bracelets, and boys at eight have their cigarettes. I came across a batch of boys returning from school one afternoon. One little fellow, apparently about seven years of age, turned out of his pockets a collection of sweets, oranges, and cigarettes, in which he indulged by turns. No one seemed to express the slightest disapproval of so small a boy smoking. The language some of these

E

little boys use is appalling, though I must admit I consider that (like the London cab-men) they are for the most part unconscious that they are using bad language at all. Games seem to be unknown to them. The only sort of play they ever take part in is leap-frog, and in this but occasionally. The Brazilian ladies get extremely fat at a very early age, from the indolence engendered by the climate. Their husbands in most cases follow suit.

Fat is regarded as a beauty, and a young girl is considered hardly marriageable unless her bones are well covered. At twenty they are rather good-looking, but later will not bear criticism. Jewellery in the form of diamonds and emeralds (especially diamonds) is worn in profusion at all times. The women would seem from the wealth of diamonds they display to wear their whole fortunes upon their persons. Indeed, to be entirely without such ornaments is regarded as not at all *comme il faut*.

Amongst the Brazilians, if one admires

anything, it is good manners for the owner to offer it to the person who expresses admiration. The worst of it is that such an offer is not always taken as an empty compliment. A young Englishman, who was not quite aware of this, was showing his handsome new watch to a Brazilian who greatly admired it. Whereupon the owner with true Brazilian politeness said that it was entirely at his friend's service, the result of which was that with a most polite bow the Brazilian pocketed the watch. On another occasion we heard of the embarrassments of a young bachelor who was roughing it at a small estancia (farm) up-country. He had been setting forth in glowing colours the many charms of his estancia to a Brazilian widow who was the mother of a numerous progeny. Upon her expressing admiration, he, in the Brazilian manner, said that it was entirely at her service. To his horror, a few days after his return, she arrived with all her children, servants, and baggage.

When travelling by the ' bond ' it is etiquette for gentlemen to pay for the tickets of

any ladies of the party, however slight may
be the acquaintanceship. At table, it is not
etiquette for a Brazilian lady to help herself to
wine until she has been offered it by a gentleman ; and this applies as between perfect
strangers. I was often forgetful of this, and
I fear many of the Brazilian ladies resented
my want of gallantry. If one borrows a small
sum of money from a Brazilian, repayment
is regarded as an insult. I was very naturally unaware of this, and when we landed at
the Isla de Flores, having no change in the
money of the country, I borrowed a dollar of
a Brazilian fellow-passenger to give to the
men who hauled up our baggage. Three days
later I procured some change, and when I,
with many thanks for his loan, tendered my
friend a dollar in repayment, he would not
take it, and appeared to be quite insulted. I
think his good feelings towards me never quite
recovered from the shock I occasioned him.

The Brazilians are a very dressy people.
The humblest of them on gala days turn out
attired in great magnificence.

Men and women who on ordinary days wear the shabbiest and dirtiest old clothes, appear on any festive occasion in the most spotless attire. We were much struck by this on board ship. Most of our Brazilian fellow-passengers made no efforts whatever to pre-serve a comely appearance during the voyage. They let their hair get frowsy, wore dirty linen and the most horrible old clothes, and generally were very much down at heel. But when we came into port, and visitors were received on board, or the passengers went on shore, toilets were made as if for a wedding. The change in their appearance might be compared to that of a butterfly issuing from the grub state. The wonder to us was, how people who could get themselves up with such perfect finish and neat-ness, could endure at other times to live in such a state of detestable grubbiness. When talking with a Brazilian of the chance of our having to undergo quarantine, he said that we should not be kept long, the third class passengers might be detained eight days, but the others would probably be let out in three.

I asked why they should make any difference.
'Oh!' was the reply, 'the first and second
class passengers only wear their shirts a
week, but the third class wear theirs a
month.' This may explain a good deal. In
their houses the place of honour is the sofa,
on either side of which, placed in most conspicuous positions, two spittoons are always to
be seen, one on each side.

Frequent complaints are heard of English
manufacturers and merchants losing their business connections with South America. This
is true enough as to all kinds of clothing and
the lighter kinds of household goods. The
reasons for the loss of the markets by Englishmen are not far to seek. It is the old difficulty
that they do not sufficiently study the requirements of the people they serve. On the whole
of our journey we met only one English commercial traveller, and, if I may be pardoned
the bull, he was a Scotchman. I found that
he could talk both Spanish and Portuguese
fluently (a necessity for a commercial traveller
in these parts), having learnt at a small expense

in some public institution in Glasgow. He was, however, travelling first class while German commercial travellers were travelling second class. The English merchants send their price lists by the ton to South America, but do not send 'travellers,' and the shop-keepers cannot buy well from mere lists, however well got up. They naturally prefer the commercial traveller with his goods, the man who will come again next year, whom they can remonstrate with personally if necessary.

The result of this want of actual contact is that our manufacturers fail to meet the real requirements of the people. The South American, living in a glorious climate, does not want clothes that will wear for ever. He wants showy, bright, cheap goods. They must be cheap, for of late the import duties have been raised to find the wherewithal to pay for railways and numerous other internal improvements. As wages and incomes have not risen with the increased taxes levied on imported manufactures, an opportunity has been afforded—mainly taken advantage of by the Germans—of producing an inferior description of goods, which, after payment of the heavy duties, can still be sold at the old prices. To facilitate the sale of these inferior articles, English makes and trade-marks have been extensively plagiarised. We came across many palpable forgeries—Royal Windsor soap of manifest German origin ; plates and cups stamped with rude travesties of the Royal arms, some with the motto misprinted as ' Honi sot qui maly pense ; ' piece goods with ' Horrocks ' clearly forged. Some English merchants say they would rather lose their trade than send out such poor stuff, but this is eminently foolish, as what is good enough for the con- suming Brazilian is surely good enough for the producing Englishman. The climate, too, as I have said, is an important consideration, and where it is ' always afternoon,' goods of the most flimsy texture will serve quite as well as if not better than goods of a much more durable description do, in a climate such as ours at home. A smart dressy people does not want things that will never wear out ; they would never be in the fashion if they had them. The exceeding desire of the Brazilians for dress is shown in the fact, of which I was assured by many who know them well, that they prefer to stint themselves in food, rather than spare money upon their garments. I am inclined to think that sham trade-marks have comparatively little to do with the success of German goods, and that the low prices, combined with the sharp pushing ways of German commercial travellers, who are thrifty and self-denying to a fault, and who, from actual contact, know the needs of the people whom they serve, are the true causes of the goods they offer meeting with a ready sale. If the English merchant is to recover lost ground, or even to hold his own, he must find inexpensive commercial travellers who will bring him into touch with distant customers. The incredibly economical and many-languaged continental 'commercial,' frugal and unwasteful in all his ways, is now 'stepping round,' and by his nimbleness ousting English merchants and English workmen from many valuable markets.

CHAPTER VII.

SANTOS TO SAN PAULO.

On our homeward voyage we landed at Santos, which lies about a day's sail south of Rio. Ships approach the harbour by a winding estuary, wooded on either bank to the water's edge. Palms and every kind of tropical vegetation grow luxuriantly in the swampy low ground. Here and there, at the foot of a lofty palm by the water's edge, we observed the rude whitewashed hovel of some black cultivator, who must, one would imagine, be ever running the gauntlet between fever and ague. Shortly after passing a little ancient fort standing on a wooded bluff, we cast anchor before Santos. The town spreads out on the low ground below the mountains, which rise range on range behind it right against the western sky.

As the sun was just going down when
the quarantine officers came off and gave us
leave to land, we decided to defer going ashore
until next day. We made arrangements for
an early start, and three of us left the ship's
side next morning as the clocks of Santos
were telling across the silent water the hour

SANTOS.

of four. The darkness was only relieved by
the faint light of the stars, Mars shining in
glorious splendour in the west. It took us full
half an hour to reach the shore. The intense
silence, which precedes the rise of the fiery
tropical sun, was unbroken save by the
rhythmic sound of the oars in the rowlocks
and their plash in the placid waters. We

reached the landing steps just as the first rays of dawn shot upward in the east. Yet but a few minutes later the town was flooded with sunlight as we walked through the streets to the station.

Though few of the inhabitants were stirring, the clean well-kept look of the streets, and the smart attractive appearance of the houses, betokened considerable prosperity. Santos is unquestionably a fortunate place; it is the port for all the great coffee district of which San Paulo is the centre. The San Paulo railway, and the large traffic it brings, has added greatly to the wealth of the people. In addition to being the port of a rich district, it enjoys the advantage of having no rivals southwards in Brazilian territory ; Santa Catharina, Porto Alegre, and Rio Grande, the only harbours to the south, having sand bars which render them inaccessible save to ships of the smallest tonnage. With such advantages it is no wonder that Santos bears outward and visible signs of the prosperity of its people. Santos and San Paulo and the other towns in the temperate latitudes of Brazil seemed to me to show clear signs of real vigorous growth, while all the cities north-wards, in tropical Brazil, seemed to have a look of flagging, as if some canker were gnawing at their vitals.

I should not mean to imply that Europeans do not thrive and thrive well in equatorial Brazil, but they must be drawn from the classes who do not labour with their hands. Coloured labour only can survive outdoor work, and coloured labour is inefficient. Europeans who lead sedentary indoor lives, the merchant and the clerk, protected from the sun's rays, may prosper greatly, if not too numerous, but they have to contend against the inertia of the coloured outdoor workers who are too easily content, and where the very 'workers' are themselves 'idlers,' there can be but a languid prosperity for the country they live in.

We arrived at the station in time, as we hoped, to get some breakfast before starting, but there was no refreshment room to be found. Luckily, outside the station there was a coffee-stall for early workmen, where black coffee and a dry roll could be obtained. As I had prudently (in case of ill-luck) brought away from the ship three eggs in my pocket, we were able, each of us, to have an egg beaten up in our coffee. But just as the beating up was proceeding before an admiring crowd of a dozen working men, a cow happened to be driven by; so, borrowing a mug from the stall keeper, we proceeded to enter into negotiations for the purchase of some milk. These terminating successfully, the cow was milked in the presence of the spectators, who watched our proceedings with keen interest and evident amusement. With this further addition to our supplies we breakfasted excellently, and were able, not only to hold out till we reached San Paulo at one o'clock, but to enjoy our journey thither, which was of real importance to us.

After running for about an hour through swampy land, mostly in cultivation and bearing the most prolific crops, interspersed with bits of tangled virgin forest, the train stopped and the engine was uncoupled. Steel ropes were attached to the carriages, and one by one they were drawn up the steep incline by fixed engines. The carriages were un-hooked and recoupled at the several landing stages with great rapidity, and forwarded one after the other from stage to stage, without any appreciable delay. Of the forest scenery, as we crept slowly up the mountain-side, I can only say that it should be seen. Our conversation was one long series of ejacu-lations of surprised delight. Here, with a soil largely composed of the richest vegetable mould, the product of the decayed vegetation of long centuries, combined with heavy dews by night and a blazing sun by day, the exu-berant growth of the trees and flowers is such as is quite undreamt of by those who know our own land only. Why do not people come and see these things—only a three weeks' voyage from our shores ? And yet they do not come. Business men and business people only as yet travel this way.

San Paulo is situated on the top of a lofty ridge in the midst of a wide elevated plateau of undulating hills. From an artistic point of view it is finely placed, but from more mundane aspects might be more conveniently situated. It is a large and thriving city, favoured with a cooler temperature than Rio and the cities further north, and surrounded by rich valleys productive of vast supplies of coffee and sugar. The streets and houses have a thoroughly business-like look. There is very little display made in the shop windows, to tempt the casual passer-by. They are rather in the nature of stores than shops, making little external show, yet able within to furnish supplies suited to the wants of, and sufficient for, a very large population. The main streets run along the crest of the ridge on which the city is built, and as one walks along them, one gets peeps through the cross streets which descend somewhat abruptly on either side of the hill, right out into the country, undulating for miles away, and bounded in the far distance by the beautiful blue mountains. The city is

well equipped with tramways, running some
miles out, of which we made good use. Built
upon a spur of the hill is the palace, now
chiefly used for Government offices. In front
lies a terraced garden with a grand overlook
upon the mountainous western plateau, and
whichever way one turns one's eyes, there
are scenes well worth gazing at. Hither in
the evening at sunset time, come young and
old, fathers and mothers, young men and
maidens, the burghers of San Paulo and their
families. And here in the balmy, mountain
air, the military band flings out its bright
music under the soft light of the new moon.

We arose at four o'clock to make the
fourteen hours' journey by rail to Rio. The
train left at six, and the carriages—the long
open cars of the United States—were well
filled ; the Brazilians dressed, as always for
a journey, in irreproachable attire.

Then came one of those transformation
scenes—common to the railways of the River
Plate alike—which are so strange at first to
the newcomer, the sudden donning of white

F

garments by the whole of the passengers.
The guard whistles, the engine gives a shriek
and a puff, and the carriages move slowly off ;
then in a twinkling the costume of civilised
life disappears as if by magic, and one finds
oneself in the midst of serried ranks of ghostly
forms clad from top to toe in spotless white
array. The effect at first is surprising and
peculiar, and, strange as it is, the cause of this
weird guise is intensely rational and a little
commonplace. It is simply a precaution
against the clouds of dust which permeate the
carriages with a persistency that nothing can
baffle. Dust penetrates every corner and every
thing. A seat left unoccupied for a few
minutes is at once covered by a thin but
very palpable layer of finely granulated par-
ticles, white, dun, buff, or red, as the geological stratum through which one passes
may chance to be. At the journey's end all
the dust-coats are put away for the next
journey, and the passengers descend in the
most perfect toilets to greet their friends. We
were running all day long through open high

rocky land, forests, and rich valleys, from San
Paulo to Rio, the valleys bearing splendid
crops of coffee, sugar, maize, and vines. At
a wayside station we purchased some fresh
sugar-cane and spent some time in gnawing
it. We found it stringy and sweet. How the
black population can find it so intensely fasci-
nating I can hardly understand. They will sit
by the hour together in a hot corner munching
away at sugar-cane, some of them becoming
little better than parasites of the plant they
devour with so much satisfaction.

For the last two hours of our journey we
were rapidly descending from the high level of
the Organ Mountains to Rio. Away in front
of us the sun was setting, and the pink and
golden hues of the mountain peaks, set round
the bay of Rio, which looked like a sapphire
in their midst, deepened into crimson and
purple as the sun went down. As we once
more alighted in Rio, the new moon like a
white pinion rose over the peak of Tijuca.

CHAPTER VIII.

SLAVERY.

BRAZIL is half as large again as Russia in
Europe, with a population only one-seventh of
that of Russia. Continental in point of size,
her population, mostly black, numbers only
12,000,000. This population is distributed
in a broad fringe along the coast, dwelling
thickly about the harbours, and becoming
sparser as one advances into the heart of the
country. Three hundred miles from the coast,
Brazil is still 'trackless Brazil,' the abode of
scattered tribes of native Indians, and for the
most part utterly unknown to the Brazilians
themselves. Owing to the population being
thus distributed, one can, without making
lengthened inland journeys, obtain very fair
data for forming some opinion as to the con-

dition of the country. What forced itself
upon my attention more than anything else,
was the marked way in which the country im-
proves as one goes southwards. The northern cities seem to be struggling to hold their
own. Humanity in equatorial Brazil seems
to be nerveless and unstrung; exhausted in
the mere effort to exist under the touch of
the flaming sword of the sun. The lassitude
of human beings was reflected in their cities ;
the sap, as it were, seemed flowing intermit-
tently and in insufficient quantity to maintain
the body politic in a healthy condition.

But as we went south the change was
very apparent. Inertia gave place to vitality ;
stagnation and decay to growth ; while the
complexion of the population shaded off by
very perceptible degrees, from black almost to
white. In the four southern provinces, which
in area are but one-twelfth of the whole of
Brazil, dwell no less than one-fourth of the
population, and that the most energetic, the
most healthy, and the most free from black
blood.

The whole fabric of Brazilian government
clearly seems to rest on these three millions
—mostly white—dwelling without, or almost
without, the tropics, and occupying but a
fragment of this vast empire ; and on their
enterprise, progress, and vitality would seem
to depend the whole future prosperity of Brazil.

The Brazilian upper classes are the descendants of Portuguese and Spanish. Life in the
tropics and a certain admixture of black blood
have not improved the race. These constitute
the landowners and the well-to-do classes.
The rest of the people either are or have until
lately been slaves, or are the not remote
descendants of slaves. The tide of European
emigration which sets to South America passes
by Brazil. Shunning all contact with the
dark-skinned half-breeds of Brazil, the white
population of Europe make as with one accord
for the River Plate. The free white will not
settle amongst the degenerate mixed breeds
of the tropics. The white of unmixed race
seems to shrink from all contact with the black
blood. A natural instinct seems to guide them

past these shores, for intermarriage of the children of the white man with the mixed race of the country is the sure penalty of halting here.

The slaves of Brazil are gradually being emancipated ; but there are still about 1,500,000 slaves in the country, most of whom are employed in the coffee plantations. As every excuse is made in order to avoid complying with the law of emancipation, it will be many years before the last slave is free. The law of emancipation is in some ways rather a doubtful boon to the slaves. For example, slaves are entitled to their freedom at sixty years of age. So that after a slave has given all the best years of his life to his employer, he is then entitled to the doubtful privilege of relying for his support upon himself for the rest of his days. This mocking way of granting freedom seems calculated to benefit the master rather than the slave. Slavery has been, and must continue to be, long after it ceases to exist as an institution, a curse to the country. Cruelty and slavery seem to be linked

together indissolubly, and emancipation does
not much mend matters, for the ill-used slave
only gives place to the idle black with his low
morals. Cruelty to slaves takes many forms,
not the least being that of feeding them upon
insufficient food of the coarsest description.
Slaves are generally fed like animals, on boiled
barley meal or beans, just tipped into a trough,
the fastest eater getting the largest share. A
new manager from the United States recently
came to a coffee plantation near Rio. He considered that the rations of the slaves were insufficient in quantity and he obtained leave
to double them. Finding that they were still
underfed for their work, he with some difficulty
obtained leave to double their rations a second
time. It was not until they had thus obtained
four times their former amount of sustenance
that they were sufficiently fed.

While we were at Rio a mistress whipped
two of her girl slaves so severely that one of
them died. The local English newspaper, com-
menting upon this barbarity, said: ' It would
seem that these two girls have been subjected

to the most barbarous tortures for the last three years, of which beatings have been the least cruel of all. One of them has died from her injuries, while the other is disfigured and injured for life. What punishment will be meted out by the authorities for these illegal and inhuman cruelties cannot easily be predicted, for it has thus far been the custom to make a pretence of investigation and then to quietly hush up the whole matter. So far as we know there is not a single case on record where a master has been punished for cruelty to his slaves.' I asked a friend who knew the country well if many slaves died of cruelty. 'Not more than one in ten,' he replied.

The dusky natives certainly suit the colouring of their surroundings better than the whites, but they are not an industrious race. As long as they have cotton enough for a garment, a little rice or maize to eat, some tobacco and maté—all of which they can obtain at a very small expenditure of labour—they are absolutely content, and nothing will induce them to further exert themselves. They do not care to use their hands at all if they can help it, and seem to regard them as merely ornamental appendages. When carrying even a cup of water, they place it upon their heads in preference to carrying it in their hands. The coffee planters have to a large extent met the diminishing supply of slave labour by additional and improved machinery; and they have been so far successful in this, that in the last seven years, although the export of coffee from Rio and Santos has risen from three million to eight million bags annually, I was assured that this increase has been accomplished without employing additional labour.

At one time an effort was made to procure Chinese labour, but the Chinese Government placed difficulties in the way and the project fell through. The need of labour, both more of it and of a better quality, is very visible in the coffee plantations. When once planted they are left too much to nature, and not properly tended. It is, as was remarked to me, 'all plantation and no cultivation.'

CHAPTER IX.

MEANS OF COMMUNICATION.

THE railways of Brazil are a subject of considerable interest to English people. They have for the most part been made by English capital, either directly or indirectly from the proceeds of loans to the Brazilian Government.

MACEIO BULLOCK WAGGON.

I think that those who know the country best will admit that, on the whole, the railways of Brazil have not been very successful ventures. The San Paulo railway is a marked success. The San Paulo and Rio railway (a

continuation of the San Paulo) has also
done well. The Dom Pedro Secundo (an ex-
tension of the same system), built and worked
by the Government, is understood to yield
very satisfactory returns; as also the Leo-
poldina line; but after making these exceptions,
the railways of Brazil, taken on their own
merits, and without having regard to the
Government guarantees, do not offer great
encouragement to investors. As they have all
been built either by the Government or by the
aid of a Government guarantee, there is every
reason why they should have been laid out
upon an intelligent plan. This unfortunately
has not been the case.

When a Government grants concessions
accompanied by valuable guarantees, thereby
assuring the building of the line guaranteed,
irrespective of its real need to the community,
every place puts in its claim for a line of railway. Pressure, political and otherwise, is
brought to bear upon the Government to grant
concessions for this place and that place;
without regard to the real commercial wants

of the country. A Ministry may be tempted to concede a guarantee for a particular line of railway in order to propitiate a particular district and gain votes. If afterwards the railway is found not to pay and not to be likely to pay, from being in the wrong place, it cannot be regarded as very surprising. I can hardly imagine more difficult ground for a Home Government to tread upon than that of guaranteeing new railway ventures in a country of such huge extent as Brazil. It would be difficult for Brazil to get her railways made without any guarantee ; for, being a mountainous country, the engineering difficulties are considerable. Still many of them ought not to have cost the sums that have been spent upon them. Railways in the Argentine Republic can be built for from 5,000*l.* to 6,000*l.* a mile, but in Brazil a fair price is from 10,000*l.* to 12,000*l.* a mile. These figures have in many cases been largely exceeded in both countries. One of the evils of the guarantee system is that, if the guaranteeing country is fairly trustworthy, investors subscribe upon

the strength of the guarantee, without considering whether the railway is likely to be a
success upon its own merits, all questions of
this kind being supposed by them to be carefully weighed by the guaranteeing Government, quite regardless of the fact that motives
other than purely business ones may have
influenced the Government when sanctioning
the guarantee. Again, when once a railway is
built and working with the assistance of a
Government guarantee, there is not the same
motive for keeping down expenses, as the
guarantee comes in to make good all defici-
encies in income. High working expenses
are not however the result solely of easily
earned guarantees, but are partly due to the
extravagant requirements of the guaranteeing
Government in the way of a numerous railway
staff. Numbers of stations in Brazil rejoice
in a station master, booking clerk, cashier,
porters, and so on, when a single porter to
load up trucks as goods come in, and attach
them to the trains, would be all that the
traffic really warrants ; passengers of course

under such circumstances being supplied with tickets by the guard of the train.

The total capital of the railways in Brazil, on which interest at the rate of from 6 to 7 per cent. has been guaranteed, amounted in 1882 to 18,000,000*l.* It is believed that it costs the Government about three-quarters of a million to meet the railway guarantees, and that it is liable for as much again upon incomplete or unmade roads. The Government has recently been cancelling somewhat arbitrarily some of these too readily granted guaranteed concessions. When it is remembered that most of the land required for the railways is obtainable for nothing, or for very moderate prices at most, it seems rather surprising to find lines costing as much as 32,000*l.* a mile.

The San Paulo Railway, the San Paulo and Rio, and the Dom Pedro Secundo, all part of one system, have succeeded, and not without reason. They go through a district extremely rich in produce and well peopled. Although the district they serve covers only about one-thousandth part of the area of

Brazil, yet within it dwells one-sixth of the
whole population of the country.

The Bahia and San Francisco railway is
a line which probably would never have been
built but for the Government guarantee
granted to gain favour with the province. It
goes through much barren country and has
cost 22,500*l.* a mile. The dividends are paid
out of the guarantee. It seems probable, however, that if the staff at unimportant stations
were reduced and the line worked on thoroughly economical principles, it would pay a
small dividend, perhaps one or two per cent.,
independent of the guarantee. It is better,
however, for Brazil to build railways that
yield no return upon the capital sunk in
making them than squander her resources
upon useless ships of war, plenty of which
may be seen rotting in the bay of Rio.

Tramways abound and are well patronised.
No one who can afford the modest ' bond '
fare thinks of walking, even a few yards.
So completely is the ' bond ' a part of existence in the towns and cities, that ' bond '

tickets are almost part of the small change of these places. They get into circulation by the conductors giving, in lieu of small change, one or more tickets for the 'bond.' These are passed from hand to hand, and in effect are a modern form of the local 'tokens' of former days. The 'bond' is really the greatest possible boon to all classes, for the roads in the towns are so rough and uneven that no feeling of dignity arising from proceeding in one's own 'shay,' can at all compensate for the incessant bumpings and joltings to which one is subjected in driving over them.

Telephones have spread over the land like gossamer threads on a September morning. Not only places of business and hotels but every private house seems to have its apparatus. I suppose one will have to grow accustomed to these things, but they certainly seem to add to the bustle and friction of life rather than to lessen toil. Telephones enable business to follow one home when the day's work should be laid aside. They brook no delay and call one away without remorse in the midst of a shave

G

or from one's soup alike. During the busy
hours of the day the shrieking of scores of
voices reverberating along the wires, makes it
impossible at times to hold audible conversation with one's interlocutor at the other end.
For communication over moderate distances,
telephones have, in South America, quite
pushed aside the telegraph.

I was much amused at watching a small
Italian boy at our hotel conversing by telephone, who, forgetting that his auditor could
not see him, gesticulated with as much vigour
as if his very expressive attitudes added force
to his words.

There is as yet no wire direct from England to South America, and telegrams have
consequently to travel round by Portugal,
which renders them costly and increases the
chances of error in transmission. This does
not, however, prevent telegrams to South
America being largely employed by English
business men, much to the disgust of many
of their ablest agents in that country. 'It is
no use thinking for oneself, as in the old days,'

more than one remarked to me ; 'we are now mere agents, told to buy one day and the next day told to hold our hands. All the thinking is done in London or Liverpool. Formerly we learnt to be merchants out here ; now we are mere clerks.'

Transit by sea to Brazil and the River Plate is carried on by a crowd of shipping companies. Thirty-five years ago the only line to Rio was the Royal Mail, which despatched one vessel a month. Those were the palmy days when 9*l.* or 10*l.* a ton was paid for freight. At the present time there are 450 steamers yearly from European ports to Brazil, and ships are glad to get freights at 1*l.* a ton. At Santos on our return we were offered a cargo of coffee to be delivered in London at 10*s.* a ton. As the Royal Mail discharges at Southampton and as the charges from Southampton to London are 7*s.* 6*d.* a ton, it is hardly necessary to say that the coffee was not shipped.

The Royal Mail company long enjoyed a monopoly of the traffic to Brazil ; but for want

of alacrity in meeting the needs of the merchants they have gradually lost the bulk of the
carrying trade, the greater share of which
seems now to have gone to Lamport and
Holt's line. The Royal Mail retain the largest
share of the passenger traffic, but have not the
happy knack of keeping abreast of the times.
If a few of their oldest directors were sent
upon a trip down the coast of Brazil, several
changes would be made which would add
greatly to the comfort of travellers.

To meet the requirements of the shipping
traffic vast sums of money have been sunk at
Rio upon quays and wharves ; unfortunately
to very little purpose. There they stand, these
costly quays with splendid steam cranes, and
every appliance, but utterly useless. Everything is taken from, and brought to, the ship's
side by lighters. Regulations of quarantine and
other troubles debar vessels from coming alongside and taking advantage of these quays.

The voyage from Rio to Lisbon usually
occupies about a fortnight. In the days of sailing vessels, the length of time required to reach

Europe was a very uncertain quantity, as for weeks together a vessel might lie with her sails flapping idly in the Doldrums. Such an undertaking was it in those days, that regular establishments were maintained in Brazil, wherein Brazilian merchants, during their absence, had their wives safely shut up under lock and key against their return.

CHAPTER X.

'YELLOW JACK.'

THE most peculiar, and in some respects the
most comical, of all our experiences, was
our incarceration as ' suspects,' on account of
yellow fever, in the Lazaretto, on the Island
of Flores, off Monte Video. We had some
suspicion that something of the kind would
befal us, but we dismissed it from our minds,
regarding it at the worst as the loss of a week
of our holiday. However, we did not escape
the unpleasant reality by merely making light
of it beforehand. We had been in the land of
yellow fever, or 'yellow Jack," as it is commonly called, and we had accordingly to pay
the penalty of a rigid quarantine. Both the
Argentine Republic and Uruguay (the Banda
Oriental) are in constant fear of its approach-

ing their shores in summer, and in order to protect and defend themselves against it, quarantine regulations are enforced against all comers from infected places. Their dread of the disease is not surprising, though I confess I think the means they adopt to baffle its coming are not exactly the best suited for the purpose. Yellow fever is to all appearance the same as bilious remittent fever—some poison which causes the bile to flow into the blood—yet somewhat akin to cholera in that it haunts localities where heat, filth, stagnant air and stagnant water, with a temperature never falling below 70 degrees all the year round, conspire together. Rio is just such a place. The sun blazes fiercely down ; no air stirs ; the temperature remains steady at 85 degrees to 95 degrees in the shade ; no tide cleanses the harbour, the rise and fall not exceeding 4 feet : putrescence of every kind heaves and simmers in the bay it never quits ; while water is insufficient in quantity for flushing the drains, so that they become active generators of disease. If the refuse was carried into the Atlantic or even left in the open for the sun and innumerable creeping things to deal with it, it would be better than for it to stagnate in the unflushed drains of the baked city emitting malignant vapours at every vent. To these contributory causes must be added the inherent laziness of the true Brazilian, begotten of his tropical existence and leading him to prefer dirt to trouble, and coupled with the indolence of the Brazilian, the utter indifference to foul surroundings of the coloured population. When all these things are so, what wonder that a hundred deaths a day and more in Rio, from yellow fever, were registered while we were there (1886)! The wonder is that the disease carried off so few, especially when it is borne in mind that just the last hot days of summer culminate in the pagan excesses of the Carnival. Of this revolting orgie which brings so many easy victims, wrecked in mind and body, into the clutch of yellow fever, a Rio paper thus writes: ' The Carnival amounts simply to this ; the waste of much time and money, the senseless masquerading of the streets in dominoes and hideous masks,

blowing trumpets, talking in falsetto voices,
and doing grotesque things which would even
shame the monkeys whom it is supposed are
being imitated by rational human beings, and
then the giving of public balls whose excesses,
indecencies and vices, are past all description.
Its excesses and vices are subversive of everything good and pure. If, however, it is permitted as a popular recreation, then why not
confine it strictly to that, and place it within
bounds which will prevent the moral and
physical injuries which result from its present
observance. It is a form of recreation which
endangers health through dangerous exposures
to the heat of a tropical summer, and which
deadens moral perceptions through the open
display of vice.'

Before 1886 the yellow fever had spared
the clean and wholesome living European
population ; but in that year they were beginning to be struck down with the rest. Like
a shower of bullets in battle no one could say
whose turn would come next. Old and young,
strong and weak, black man and white man,

no one knew how soon he might be called away. The suddenness with which it summons its victims is the terrible side. One apparently in the full vigour of life may be struck down in the morning and before sundown have passed into the very tomb. More like death in battle than the peaceful and quiet summons to die we know at home. So rapid is the burial that friends do not even gather at the grave-side, the custom being for all burial services to be held at the grave the day-week following death. Of all sights, few perhaps are sadder than a plague-smitten ship. When we left Rio, several lay in the Bay dismanned. Everyone on board, from captain to cabin-boy, dead of yellow fever. But for this terrible disease Rio would be a very paradise; and yet it would seem that with cleanliness she might cease to be a pest-house. That cleanliness can exorcise this woful disease is evident from the experience of New Orleans during the abolition war. New Orleans had long been the abiding home of yellow fever and a very charnel-house. General Butler captured the city and occupied it with several thousand troops for a long period. The North raised an outcry, declaring that he was destroying his men. But he set his soldiers to cleanse the city. The sewers were cleaned, and every slum and hole and cranny. Refuse of all kinds was destroyed, and severe penalties were attached to any unclean ways. Yellow fever left the city and only gradually returned some years after the occupation was over. Rio, it seems, has taken warning from the repeated visitations of yellow fever, and especially from the widespread mortality of 1886, and has so far stirred herself as to be able to present a clean bill of health in this respect during the past season (1887), no doubt assisted therein by the fact that those most prone to the disease have been carried to untimely graves.

This much is necessary to explain the precautions taken in the River Plate against yellow fever, and our consequent relegation to a lazaretto.

CHAPTER XI.

THE LAZARETTO.

WE cast anchor off the Isla de Flores, fifteen
miles from Monte Video, at seven o'clock on a
Tuesday morning. My wife and I were the
only two first-class passengers who had come
from Rio. All the others had come through
from ports beyond, and so might quarantine on
board the ship in the River Plate—irksome,
but nothing more. Our only chance of avoiding quarantine on the island was that the
lazaretto might be so full that we could not
be taken in.

The Isla de Flores is a mere strip of rock,
rising at most twenty feet above the sea level.
It is about three-quarters of a mile long, and
its average width is about two hundred yards.
The only buildings on the island are a light-

house and a lazaretto. Moored alongside us was
another large steamer, which had arrived the
day before. We soon learnt that the lazaretto
was full, and that there would be no room
for us until the next morning ; this seemed like
a reprieve. It might be that we should be
allowed to quarantine on board after all ; but
no such luck awaited us. At eight o'clock
next morning, just as I was taking my final
nap and trying to forget the proximity of

ISLA DE FLORES.

Flores Island, we were hurried breakfastless
on shore to taste the unknown delights of
quarantine. We were crammed like herrings
into the boat, grease was on the seats, bilge
water was flopping about, horrid little yapping
dogs, pets of the emigrants, were rushing con-
tinually between our legs, the Spanish and
Italian emigrants were all talking at the top
of their voices, volubly expressing their disgust

at the ill-treatment of their boxes and other belongings, parrots were screeching, and a hot sun was pouring its vertical rays mercilessly upon us. However, the journey to the shore was soon over; we stepped ashore, our boxes were banged down anyhow, and there we were in durance. After much chatter on the part of the untidy, not to say ragged officials, our baggage was loaded in a very leisurely fashion upon a truck, and pushed up to the airing ground which stands about a hundred yards from the landing pier, immediately outside the walls of the court of the lazaretto. The airing ground is distinguished by a quantity of iron pens, much like those in which sheep are enclosed at markets, extending over about an acre. The object of the pens is to separate the passengers, affording them at the same time rails whereon they may hang out their goods to bake in the sun and air in the breeze.

The airing immediately commenced. We were instructed to ransack our boxes to the depths and hang out and spread about all their contents. There were at least one hundred of us all doing the same thing, and the sight was truly comical. It looked for all the world like an old German fair. The clothes-clad railings had much the appearance of booths, and the varied costumes displayed to an admiring crowd—for we all investigated each other's belongings, the women taking the lead—gave quite the appearance of an active trade being carried on. It was all done, too, in the most grave and sedate fashion, as if we had been accustomed to the business from our earliest days. The novelty of a mutual inspection of goods gradually wore off as the days went on, and the favourite attitude after our box was emptied, was that given in the illustration. As we

were out in the full blaze of the morning sun, this use of the family trunk afforded some shade to the body, and at the same time a

camping ground fairly free from insects.
After the first two days, there was a good
deal of make-believe about the unpacking,
although we had to rigidly adhere to the
two hours' airing of a morning, from eight
to ten o'clock, as long as we were upon the
island.

After our first morning's two hours' airing,
we were taken off to our cells. My wife and
I were fortunate in getting a small room to
ourselves ; if the first-class passengers had
been more numerous, we should have been
most certainly separated, and packed away
anyhow, as the second-class passengers were,
with people of all nationalities, perhaps compelled to share a bed as well as a room, with
other horrors of all descriptions. Luckily, we
were spared this experience, and only learned
how these things were, from an unfortunate
English couple, who had to endure these additional miseries as best they could in the second-
class corridor. Our cell was a small whitewashed apartment about twelve feet square,
up one flight of stairs, and opened upon a

long corridor. It was much like a room in a
workhouse, only not so clean. At the end of
the corridor, upon which our room opened,
was the eating room. The second-class passengers in similar rooms below slept six in a
room, and the third-class passengers had two
long chambers, one for each sex, and slept on
palliasses on the ground, having their meals on
trestle tables in the yard. We made our own
beds, and generally did the work of the house!
We found it rather difficult, however, to perform our new duties to our satisfaction, as the
broom we had the use of, was worn to a
stump, and would not do its work efficiently;
moreover, we had no blacking for our boots.
The sheets of the beds, too, were not what they
might have been; as far as we could make out
from the marks upon them, they seemed to
have done duty first as table-cloths, and then,
when too much soiled to present a comely
appearance on the table, took a turn, on the
way to the washtub, as sheets for the beds.
This economy in washing was probably due to
the fact that the only water on the island fell

from the clouds, and as rain had not fallen for
a long period, water was not to be wasted in
unnecessary washings. How scarce and valuable it was we well knew, for immediately
under our window was the water-tank, a large
chamber underground hewn out of the rock,
and vaulted over with brick. As ill luck
would have it, a large staple was affixed
to the wall just outside our window to carry
the wheel on which ran the chain by which
buckets were lowered into the water-tank.
It creaked and groaned with rust and age
in a perfectly maddening way, and as most
of the water was drawn up in the very early
morning, the days, which were long enough,
were still further drawn out, by our being
awakened by the hideous squeaks and groan-
ings of the well-chain. The day before we
left the island, the water in the tank came to
an end. As there were only a few inches remaining in the bottom, the officials appeared
to think it a good opportunity to clean out
the tank, so proceeded to empty it. The
emptying process gave us much amusement.

Every old bucket, bottle, and biscuit tin, in
fact everything that could be pressed into the
service, was carefully filled with the precious
fluid which was ladled up from the depths—
water it could hardly be called, for, thick in
colour at the commencement, it soon became
more solid than liquid, and violently pungent
to the nose. When it reached this stage the
officials held a consultation, and after some
consideration decided to condemn it as unfit
for use ; but, instead of removing it to a distance, they emptied it out upon the ground
immediately above the reservoir, so that all
this delightful mess could not fail to permeate
the ground, and again pollute the fresh supply
of water. Whilst this entertainment was
going forward, the official in charge kept
gesticulating to us to retire from our window,
evidently not caring for our supervision. We
were much amused at his holding his nose
and intimating how ill we should make ourselves if we remained at the window.

The real hardships of the lazaretto were
the unsavoury food and unsavoury smells.

We were given black coffee and sour bread
every morning before the clothes parade.
There was butter too, but it was quite uneat-
able. Milk was an extra, costing 8s. a pint.
After the airing of garments was over, we
had déjeuner, with oily soup and various
chunks of hard meat cooked in oil, about as
tough and gristly as the hardest india-rubber ;
some very repulsive vegetables, an apple each,
vin ordinaire, and black coffee. Dinner at five
was somewhat more ample as far as food went,
but not more palatable. Our meals were one
prolonged groan from beginning to end from
the five partakers thereof; three of the second-
class passengers having paid extra to share
the comparative comforts of the upper corridor.
Yet we did not hurry over them ; the waiter
did—not hurry ; the cook did—not hurry ; in
fact no one hurried, for there was nothing to
hurry for ; there was no place of amusement
to betake ourselves to nor anything to do. The
only vestige of amusement we could extract
from our dinner arose from the erratic times
at which the pudding appeared, often at the

beginning, sometimes in the middle, but never at the end. Once we tried a very lean and hungry chicken, for which, being an extra, we paid 8s. The only satisfactory extras we indulged in were poached eggs at 10d. a piece. There were a few geese running on the island, and we asked whether we might have one as an 'extra.' 'No,' was the reply, 'they are kept for the invalids.' Poor invalids—what a prospect!

On the third day of our quarantine matters in the food line brightened a little, for some kind friends sent us some potted meats, jams, wine, and grapes from Monte Video. The officials thought the grapes too good for us; so they appropriated them. However the pâté de foie gras and the preserved peaches reached us, and though they were not exactly the sustenance we most required, they did duty fairly well.

In case of supplies of food running short, a few ragged, lean, hungry-looking sheep were kept on the island. On the day before we left, supplies ran short, and it became necessary to kill a sheep. The first thing to do was to catch it, and in so small a place this seemed to be an easy thing enough. However, after several men had spent quite half an hour chasing the sheep to no purpose,

LIGHTHOUSE, FROM OUR WINDOW IN THE LAZARETTO.

they brought out a lasso. I thought it would be all over with the sheep then, but another half hour slipped away and still the sheep was at large. As the sheep was absolutely necessary, and there was no other way of capturing it, a gun was brought out, and with

much solemnity the poor brute was deliberately
shot.

The window of our chamber looked out
upon the lighthouse, but we were not allowed
to go there. From the doorway, on the oppo-

COURT OF THE LAZARETTO.

site side of our room, we looked across the
yard, as shown in the above illustration. The
treble-gabled building at the extremity of the
island, about one-third of a mile away, is the
hospital, and on the other side of the hospital,

and in fact forming a sort of garden to it, is the cemetery. While we were in the lazaretto a brig came in with a small-pox patient on board. The poor fellow was immediately placed inside a long wooden box a trifle larger than a coffin, and carried by four men very slowly from the pier to the hospital. The ground is so uneven that they could only go at a snail's pace, and under a semi-tropical sun the temperature of the dark box must have been something frightful. Landed at the hospital with the cheerful cemetery as the only prospect from the windows, the patients see no doctors, for they do not visit the patients, for fear of infection, but prescribe by telephone.

We were somewhat fortunate in being allowed to prowl down to the cemetery during the first four days of our incarceration, for the hospital being then empty, they did not mind our going that way. This was a great comfort, for in the immediate vicinity of the lazaretto the smells of putrid and decaying substances made it most unpleasant to loiter there.

From the little pier they might pitch all their
refuse into deep water, but instead of so disposing of it, they scatter it broadcast about on
the rocky ground. As there are no birds and
scarcely any insects on the island, save a very
small kind of ant and certain human pests,
nature does not do the scavenging, and the result is a hideous litter, and repellent odours
which the sea breezes stir, but cannot over-
come. One could not help feeling that the
life we had to lead was eminently calculated
to develop, if not to generate, sickness and
disease.

We were, according to promise, to reckon
the lay day on board our steamer as one of
the six days of our quarantine; we expected
to get away from the island on the fifth day
after landing. We accordingly distributed
among our fellow-travellers so much of the
food sent us from Monte Video as we did
not need, reserving just enough to finish at
breakfast on the morning of the fifth day.
That morning the emigrants and the Brazilians, according to their wont on state occa-

sions, arrayed themselves in their utmost
splendour, some of the costumes of the peasants being most picturesque. We all sat
down, everyone on his own box, ready for
the tug-boat to take us away. But an ugly
rumour went round that the lay day on board
the steamer was not to be reckoned. It
proved to be only too true—the elegant
toilets had been made in vain; alas! too,
we had no more eatable food left; it was all
gone, and there was another hideous twenty-
four hours to be made out. Never did we feel
more truly the sickness of heart arising from
hope deferred. The true reason of our deten-
tion undoubtedly was that the lazaretto was
not full, and they were making 20l. a day by
keeping us!

This was but a natural result of the lazaretto being farmed out; the Government letting it, so I was informed, for 200l. a year—a
highly profitable arrangement for the takers.
Next day we really got off, but we did not
believe we were going till the whistle was
given and the screw began to turn. The sea

was a bit lumpy, and I was quite sorry for our splendidly attired fellow-travellers, for they got several splashings and partial drenchings before we were alongside the quay in Monte Video. Then began the most deafening appeals from a surging throng of porters and boatmen, who swooped down upon us and seized every package they could lay hold of. It was a wild scene of scream and scramble, but we were prepared for it beforehand, and by organising with our fellow-passengers a system of piquets, we protected our goods and got them safely on shore. The first thing we did on landing was to indulge in the luxury of having our boots blacked, a process they had not undergone for a full week past. Then, as all others I believe do under similar circumstances, we made for the best hotel and ordered a good but simple meal, to which we did the justice that only half-famished mortals can.

. CHAPTER XII.

UP STREAM.

AFTER the meal was over which celebrated
our deliverance from captivity, we proceeded
by the 'bond' over a portion of the sixty miles
of tramways, which serve the 120,000 inhabitants of the city of Monte Video.

BIT OF MONTE VIDEO FROM THE SEA.

The capital of the Banda Oriental is unquestionably a fine city. It caused me no
little surprise to find that so young a city
could well bear comparison with many an
ancient European city. No amount of ex-
planation will quite get over one's very

natural astonishment at finding, in a new and
distant land, cities which in every point can
measure themselves against old cities with
centuries of growth. Uruguay was passing
through a revolutionary struggle at the very
moment we landed, yet to the eye of a
stranger looking at the city and the quiet
stream of business that was going forward,
there was nothing whatever to indicate that
the country was in the throes of a revolution.
We were much amused when at Buenos Ayres
two days later (only sixty miles distant), to
read an account in one of the newspapers of
the miserable plight of Monte Video. The
writer of the article, after describing in dismal
colours the progress of the revolution, con-
cluded by stating that in Monte Video 'business was at a standstill, the shops and
merchants' stores were closed, and grass was
growing in the streets.' This is a delightful
illustration of the way in which, without any
justification, alarming and unfounded reports
are spread, the only effect of which is to
assist the ' bears ' of various securities. Such

a statement, emanating from such a source,
would to the mind of an ordinary English
reader appear perfectly trustworthy, though
in reality utterly fallacious.

Monte Video, like Lisbon, lies stretched
out on a long hill-side, and presents an imposing appearance when approached by water.
To the left of Monte Video, as seen from
the sea, rises the Cerro, about 500 feet high,

THE CERRO.

crowned by a lighthouse. From this hill,
the 'green hill,' the city obtains its name of
Monte Video. Though the cupolas and mina-
rets of the churches make a show at a little
distance from the city, Monte Video cannot be
regarded as a 'churchy' place. The cathedral
is nothing more than a big church of a very
average kind. The others are few in number,
and, with the single exception of the Church

of the Immaculate Conception, they are all architecturally poor in quality. The best buildings are the Opera House and the Exchange, while the Post Office, Custom House, Law Courts, and University are decidedly effective.

The cathedrals and churches in Brazil, Uruguay, and the Argentine Republic (save at Cordova), give one the impression that religion, in its outward forms and ceremonies at any rate, occupies a very unimportant position. In many places one comes across churches which, after being partially built, have been abandoned unfinished, while elsewhere many of the churches, though finished, are manifestly stunted in growth. The proportion of priests to the population must be very small, judging from the very few one meets with in public places, and from the stories which are current of districts visited by the priest at most once in five years, when he has a busy time christening big children and completing, with church rites, ex-post-facto marriages and burials. Large tracts of land in Brazil and in the Argentine Republic, most of which is of high quality, were formerly in the possession of various religious orders. For some years past these orders have been forbidden to enrol new members, and these countries are gradually resuming possession of the properties.

Monte Video is fortunate in having a supply of good building stone within easy reach, while Buenos Ayres has to fetch every cubic inch of stone from either Entre Rios, or the Banda Oriental, or from 200 miles inland. The harbour of Monte Video on the map appears to be big enough to float all the navies of the world, and, were the depth of water sufficient, its area would be ample for that purpose. The harbour is, however, unfortunately very shallow. The consequence is that the big ocean-going ships have to lie quite far out at sea, a mile at least from the city of Monte Video, exposed to the full beat of the strong south-easterly gales. The inconvenience of this to passengers is great, and the cost of sending cargo by lighters to and fro from ship to shore is very serious. This will be understood when I say that it not unfrequently happens that the cost of landing cargo at Monte Video (and at Buenos Ayres likewise) equals in amount the freight charged for the whole voyage from England. This must needs be a very serious tax upon the consumer and a great impediment to trade. A scheme is on foot to build a breakwater and harbour for Monte Video at a cost of 3,000,000*l*. It is certain that if Monte Video desires to continue to rival Buenos Ayres as a port she will have to make proper provision for the protection of shipping and for the easy discharge of cargo. Buenos Ayres is making great strides in this direction, and before long will offer shipping very great advantages, with every facility for large vessels to discharge alongside the quays.

Monte Video offers to merchants one immense advantage in that the custom-house regulations are far ahead of those of Buenos Ayres. There is much less red-tape at the Monte Video custom-house, and, what is even more important, cargo is handled there as

I

if it might be injured by rough treatment; while at Buenos Ayres goods are knocked about as if they were made of something considerably stronger than adamant. So badly are packages treated at Buenos Ayres that I have been told that it is better to send some classes of goods direct to Rosario, and then forward them on to Buenos Ayres, a return journey by train of 186 miles, than submit them to the mercies of the Buenos Ayres custom-house officials.

From Monte Video steamers ply up the Uruguay and Paraguay rivers. There are two different steamship companies, one English and one French, and their steamers are all that could be desired. They are splendidly appointed in every way, and are equal to the best of the pleasure steamers on the Clyde. The food is excellent. I found they kept two cooks on each boat; one devoted his attention entirely to pastry, of which the Brazilians are extremely fond. These cooks are better paid than English curates, getting 3l. a week and all found. We left Monte Video by one of these steamers at six in the evening, and crossed to Buenos Ayres, where we arrived at daybreak. Thence we proceeded up the river to Salto. My wife came into our cabin shortly after we had started and found me combing my hair with a comb which I was under the impression belonged to her. She pronounced it to be a filthy, dirty old comb, and for fear of further accidents she calmly flung it out of the window to rejoice the mermaids. A few days later we were on another steamer, and to our surprise there was another comb no better than the one that went out of the cabin window. So we came to the conclusion that they were there free of charge, to enable the natives to make an impromptu toilet when they carried no baggage. Some of the hotels being of a generous turn of mind, provide a clothes-brush in addition, but they none of them seem to rise to a tooth-brush; perhaps the everlasting wooden tooth-pick which is plied vigorously after every meal by women and men alike may be taken to do duty instead.

When we got into the Uruguay River the drinking water in the water-bottles placed on the tables assumed a brownish tinge. There is no sediment in the water, but the brown colour gave it a distinctly unwholesome appearance. On inquiry we found that the water, far from being injurious, was regarded as especially good, the colour it carries coming from large beds of sarsaparilla through which it flows much further up stream.

The River Plate is so wide at Buenos Ayres that the opposite side (the Uruguay side) cannot be seen. As will be seen by a reference to the map, Buenos Ayres lies almost at the end of the River Plate. Within a very short time after leaving Buenos Ayres we passed the fortified island of Martin Garcier, which commands the entrances to the rivers Paraná and Uruguay. After leaving Martin Garcier the wide waters rapidly contract and the banks rise now and again more than two hundred feet above the river, many a picturesque wooded bluff standing out along the river course. Dotted about on the hillsides

are the numerous estancias (cattle farms) of
the prince farmers of Uruguay, many of the
farm buildings alone covering a considerable
acreage. These riverside estancias have a
high value from being upon the great waterway, which brings both friends and customers.
One often hears that the great estancieros are
too well off, and there is much truth in this.
Their estates are so large that they produce
all, and more than all, that their owners need.
So things are let go on in a sleepy way, the
natural increase in flocks and herds being
sufficient for their needs, little effort being
made to improve the breeds of sheep and
cattle or to colonise and cultivate their broad
lands. Many of the estancieros of Uruguay
are English, and these are amongst the most
enterprising, having done more than others
to rail off their lands into paddocks, which
is the first step to improving the breed by
separating the various kinds and classes of
cattle and sheep.

The furthest point to which steamers can
proceed on the Uruguay River is Salto (the

'falls'), as here begin the rocks and rapids which for the next one hundred miles render the river impassable, except at very unusual seasons of flood. The Brazilian Government keep some small gunboats on the upper waters of the River Uruguay, and some time ago two of these gunboats waited for three years at Salto before a river flood gave them an opportunity of proceeding up stream. The navigation of the Uruguay River from Buenos Ayres to Salto is here and there difficult owing to sunken rocks, which are a peril when the river is low. The Uruguay and Argentine Governments are supposed to buoy all the dangerous places and charge a pilotage tax for doing so ; but, though they charge the tax, they so inefficiently do the work, that the steamboat companies have to pay both the tax and also for getting the work done privately, otherwise the river would not be properly buoyed ; whereat they naturally grumble in a quiet way.

CHAPTER XIII.

REVOLUTION.

WE reached Salto about ten days after leaving Monte Video, having been delayed at Buenos Ayres for a week, owing to the interruption of the river traffic, due to the revolution ˙in progress on the north-west frontier of Uruguay. We took our passage in the 'Cosmos,' and, owing to the local disturbances, we had this fine vessel almost entirely to ourselves. We reached Salto at midday on a Friday, and took up our quarters at the Hotel Concordia, a large modern hotel built in the centre of the city, where they made us very comfortable. The first sight that we saw after our arrival in the city was the entrance of a large body of prisoners, in pitiable plight, straight from the field of battle. As we were more or less in

the thick of the turmoil for the next ten days,
and had full opportunity of learning all par-
ticulars about what had happened and was
happening, I will here briefly narrate what
we learnt concerning this attempted revolution, as it may in some degree serve to show
how far the danger of revolution may still
be numbered as amongst the risks to the
future progress of these countries.

For more than a year before the revolution
actually broke out, subscriptions were being
collected, arms provided, and all other necessary preparations made. Drilling had been
going on in Buenos Ayres and elsewhere on
the Argentine side daily for three months
before the revolutionists crossed the River
Uruguay. The outbreak of hostilities was
for months so likely to occur at any moment
that all along the river trade was utterly para-
lysed. No one would make any purchases,
and stores of all kinds were depleted to the
utmost, through fear of military requisitions.

Within quite recent times revolutionary
movements have been known to terminate

successfully which in the beginning consisted of nothing but a few scores of armed horsemen banded together, who fed themselves at the expense of the estancieros, and who kept out of the way of the Government troops by hard riding until they had attracted sufficient numbers to their side to take the offensive with success. The revolutionary movement of 1886, however, started under much more favourable conditions. The revolutionists were able to place no less than 1,500 well-armed soldiers at once in the field, who had been drilled for months. They possessed, moreover, a battery of artillery. Is it any wonder, then, that the people of the Banda Oriental, three-fourths of whom favoured the revolutionists, regarded the coming revolution as already an assured success ?

To make the position of the revolutionists clear, it is necessary to refer to the little map here given. The revolutionists were encamped in the Argentine province of Entre Rios, chiefly about Monte Caseros. The East Argentine line runs from Ceibo to Concordia, and

between these two places the River Uruguay,
owing to rapids, is useless for purposes of
navigation. On the opposite side of the river,
in the Banda Oriental, from Salto to Isla

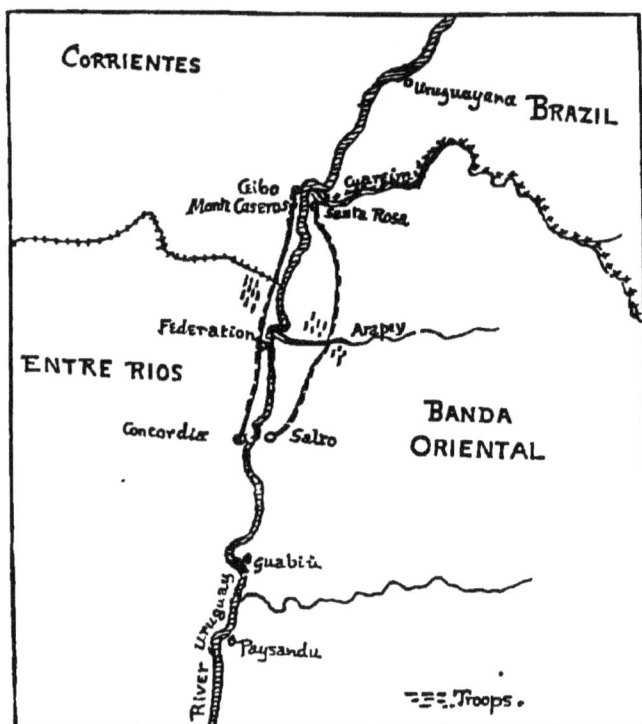

Cabellos (just beyond the Arapey) extended
the North Western of Uruguay Railway (now
terminating at the Cuareim River). Down the
river below Concordia on the Entre Rios side,
and below Salto on the Banda Oriental side,

no railway runs, but below these places the river is navigable.

The East Argentine Railway does not extend up the river beyond Ceibo, but from Ceibo the river again becomes navigable. For purposes of revolution, as against Uruguay, however, this upper portion of navigable river is of little service, for as the Banda Oriental terminates at the Cuareim River, troops coming down stream would have no choice but to land at Santa Rosa. If they succeeded in effecting a landing here, which would be difficult, as the exact point of their disembarkation would be known, they would be subject to all the additional risks attendant upon being hemmed in at the start, in the most remote corner of the country.

From January to the end of March 1886, the insurgent forces were encamped on the Argentine side in Entre Rios. As the harbour offered to these enemies of the national government of the Banda Oriental had become a scandal and a transparent breach of international amity, the Argentine Govern-

ment felt compelled to inform the revolutionists that they could no longer remain
encamped in Entre Rios, face to face with
the country they were preparing to invade.
They were further informed that the Argentine Government would send troops to compel
them to retire into Corrientes, which is the
next province up the river, and lies opposite
to the Brazilian frontier. This notification
brought matters to a crisis. To have withdrawn into Corrientes would have been fatal
to all hope of success. It would have left
the revolutionists with only Santa Rosa to
make a descent upon, for the rapids below
this point render it impossible to drop further
down stream for purposes of effecting a landing elsewhere. Moreover, in the upper reaches
of the river above Ceibo, there is very little
shipping of any kind obtainable, either by
payment or by force. It, therefore, became
urgently necessary to commence the revolution forthwith, or abandon it ignominiously.

The Revolutionary Committee took coun-
sel with General Arredondo, who was in

command of the insurgent forces, and he
reported to them that, although he could not
advise the attempt being made, he was prepared to lead his little army across the river
into the territory of the Banda Oriental, if
they gave him orders to do so. The reply of
the Revolutionary Committee to this not very
cheering offer of their general was an order to
invade. General Tajes (now President of the
Banda Oriental), who was in command of the
troops of the Republic, was under the impression that the attempt to cross the Uruguay
River would most likely be made just where
the Arapey River runs into it ; for news had
reached him that the invasion was now only a
matter of days, and he knew that the insurgent
forces were encamped between Federacion and
Monte Caseros opposite the Arapey. General
Tajes accordingly withdrew his troops by rail
from Salto, and posted them strongly about
the Arapey. General Arredondo, on the
other hand, skilfully matured his plans for
invading the Banda Oriental, so that he might
enter with his full force, and at the same time

without encountering the enemy. By en-
camping his little army near Federacion,
a long way above Salto, he not only led
General Tajes to suppose that the invasion
would be attempted in the neighbourhood of
the Arapey, so that the defending forces were
wholly withdrawn from Salto, but he also
lulled to sleep the fears of the owners of the
steamboats which ply from Monte Video and
Buenos Ayres to Salto, and which generally
accumulate at Salto on Sundays.

Circumstances being so far favourable to
the revolutionists, a bargain was struck with
the East Argentine Railway Company to
convey the 1,500 insurgents for a sum of
10,000 dollars (1,500*l.*) from Monte Caseros
to Concordia (a mile below Salto on the opposite bank of the river) during the night of
Saturday, April 3. Thus it was that early
on Sunday morning, April 4, the little army
found themselves at Concordia. Salto, almost
opposite, lay unprotected, and in the river
before them were moored three large passenger
steamers. There was nothing to prevent the

insurgents either from seizing Salto or em-
barking on the steamers and making a descent
on some other place lower down the river. It
was an anxious moment for those in Salto,
who, from the tops of their houses, could see
all that was happening at Concordia. They
were naturally afraid that the destination of
the revolutionists was Salto, for there had
been rumours that they intended to take and
hold the town. And as the city, which is of
considerable size, the third largest city in the
kingdom, containing stores of every kind, was
now denuded of troops, the opportunity for
the revolutionists seemed to have come. It
is extremely likely that the insurgent forces
would have seized Salto had it not been for
the prudent foresight of the manager of the
North Western of Uruguay Railway, who had
asked for and obtained a small guard to protect each of the bridges and culverts on the
company's line. The revolutionists had, on
the preceding Saturday, sent across the river
a small force of men to blow up these culverts and bridges, but when they approached

them they found that each one was guarded by about ten soldiers, and as the scouts sent over to perform this duty could only move about the country by twos and threes, they were not sufficiently strong to attempt any attack upon the guards of the bridges. · Had they been able to effect their purpose, they could have delayed considerably the return of the Government troops to Salto, and so given the revolutionary forces some breathing-time after landing.   But as the bridges were intact, and the insurgents were not prepared to precipitate an immediate conflict with the enemy, the only thing left for them to do was to seize the steamers which lay in the river, embark their forces, and drop down the stream to effect a landing elsewhere.

So the many anxious watchers on the flat-topped houses of Salto were spared the horrors of a battle in their midst.   They saw the revolutionists embark, and the steamers one by one depart.   A landing was effected at Guabiù, fifty miles below Salto, and after months of preparation the revolutionists were at last in the enemy's country, well supplied with arms and ammunition and artillery, but with nothing more.

They were without food, and they had as yet to obtain possession of 1,000 horses promised them in the Banda Oriental. These horses they never obtained, for the estanciero near Salto who had agreed to provide them, betrayed the

VIEW OF CREEK WHERE INSURGENTS LANDED.

insurgents at the last moment, drove off his horses, and left only a steward in possession, the blowing out of whose brains did not furnish the unfortunate invaders with the much-needed horses. The effort to obtain these horses on which they depended so much, led them to strike northwards from Guabiù in the direction of Salto. They might have gone

K

southwards to Paysandù—a large and wealthy city which lay close by—and taken it without a struggle, for no troops were there. But they went on a fool's errand instead, after the horses which they were never to get.

The difference between the invaders and the troops of the Banda Oriental was very marked. The revolutionists were largely drawn from merchants' and lawyers' offices in Monte Video and Buenos Ayres, and were not at all the equals of the regular troops in point of physique. In matter of discipline, too, they could not compare with the soldiers of Uruguay. We saw a large body of the latter arrive at Salto from the Arapey by train, and their steadiness and discipline were evident from the silence, regularity, and dispatch with which they got into and out of the carriages, although such a mode of travelling must, in all probability, have been utterly new and strange to most of them.

The long straight street of Salto on Monday morning, April 5, presented a very remarkable appearance. It was filled from end to end

by 2,000 foot soldiers harnessing and equipping for service a multitude of horses of every
kind and description—soldiers many of whom
had evidently never ridden a horse before; but
the useful little docile animals, standing some
$14\frac{1}{2}$ hands high, were somehow got underneath
the Tommy Atkins of the Banda Oriental,
and when mounted he managed to remain in
the saddle. Horses were pressed in from all
quarters, every horse in the country being at
the disposal of the Government in time of war.
An unfortunate milkman, who, ignorant of
what was happening, rode into the town with
his milk-cans dangling at his horse's sides, was
summoned to hand over his horse instanter.
Instead of submitting, he clapped spurs to its
flanks, and made a bolt for it. But a well-
mounted orderly gave chase and soon had
the milkman by one leg, when without any
ado he hoisted him out of his saddle, and,
leaving him shaken and sprawling on the
ground, grasped his horse by the reins and
trotted off with it for active service in the
field. By three o'clock in the afternoon

Salto had resumed its usual appearance, the soldiers having by this time completed their preparations in a thoroughly businesslike manner, and set out on their march to the field of battle.

The invaders, meanwhile, were in a sad plight. Without horses and without supplies, they were neither in a condition to fight nor were they able to keep out of the way of fighting. The revolutionists came into contact with the regular troops on Monday evening (April 5), and some slight skirmishing took place. On the following day, Tuesday, the regular troops attacked the revolutionists in some force, but were repulsed. On Wednesday morning the regular troops, under the command of General Tajes, were in considerable force all round the revolutionists, outnumbering them by about five to one. The revolutionists (all but a few score of them) were on foot, thoroughly wearied with continual marching, want of sleep, and want of food. Soon after sunrise the battle began. The regular troops began with artillery fire, which had no great effect save that of dispiriting the revolutionists, who could not reply. For, although they had with infinite labour (being short of horses) brought their park of artillery into action, they found it was only a white elephant; and after killing ten of their own men in the effort to use their guns, they discarded them. Then the regular troops were thrown out in skirmishing order, and worked their way forward with steadiness and precision, making heavy play amongst the revolutionists, who were not equally well handled. The battle ended after some four hours' fighting, the revolutionists being gradually beaten down in the conflict. Three hundred of the revolutionists—many of them sons of the best families in the Banda Oriental—were amongst the slain and wounded. Six hundred were taken prisoners, and the rest made their escape from the field. Some succeeded in crossing the frontier of Brazil, after a long and weary journey, while others were captured later on in small detachments.

The national guards had been called out

to support the regular troops. The national guards—the militia of the country—are the gauchos (native peasants) of the Banda Oriental, mounted on their own horses, clad in their ordinary dresses—brown poncho, loose baggy trousers with a waist-belt bristling with weapons, wearing broad scarlet ribbons round their greasy hats to distinguish them as soldiers. They look uncommonly like banditti, and as soldiers are really quite useless, but are useful as guides and aides-de-camp. They were supposed to take an active part in the fighting, but as their sympathies were all on the side of the revolutionists, they at first held quite aloof, biding their time to take sides with the enemy. When, however, the battle of Guabiù had been fought and lost, by the insurgents, the national guards, losing their sympathies for the enemy in their desire for booty, set about cutting the throats of the wounded and plundering the slain in a way that had to be rather roughly restrained. With the exception of some foreigners, who were taken prisoners, and who being unable to

show any claim to being in any way 'Orientals,' were shot on the field, the revolutionists were treated with the utmost consideration.

The means adopted for disposing of the
slain were simple and original. They threw
lassos over the dead, dragged the bodies to
some convenient hollow in the ground,

GAUCHO LASSOING THE DEAD.

scattered a few spits of earth over them,
and the sepulture was complete. Ten days
elapsed before the last of the prisoners were
brought into Salto. Meanwhile the main
body of them had been sent down to Monte
Video, and entertained at a banquet given by

General Santos. On his dismissing them with a free pardon they cheered him, yet many of them went straight to Buenos Ayres to begin plotting against him again. The revolutionists explained their failure in a very satisfactory manner to themselves, fondly imagining that had they obtained their 1,000 horses they could have turned the fortunes of war. They might no doubt have prolonged matters a little, by keeping out of the way of the regular troops, but the end must have been the same. The fencing in of the estancias has made it by no means easy for a considerable body of troops to move about. With iron fences in all directions, it is a matter of difficulty to move at all at night, and quite impossible to move with dispatch, while by day the movement of troops over the open rolling plains can be seen at great distances. Telegraphs, railways (though at present the Banda Oriental is very insufficiently provided with them), and artillery, give the regular troops of the country overwhelming advantages. The revolution of 1886 is really nothing less than a knock-down blow for revolutionists. Other means must be found for ridding the country of objectionable rulers.

Thus it was that, on our coming to Salto, the first sight we saw was a long cavalcade of soldiers and national guards in charge of a large number of the most scrubby, miserable, dejected-looking wretches one ever would wish to see. Following the cavalcade came a train of waggons containing the wounded, who uttered groans as the great lumbering spring-less vans, each drawn by eight or ten horses, jolted horribly over the rough road. The streets were thronged, but dead silence reigned, for the sympathies of the people were with the beaten revolutionists.

It is very fortunate that the revolution failed so completely, for it is scarcely possible to estimate the evil effects of such disturb-ances upon the people of the country in the districts affected. As illustrating the lawless conditions it fosters, I may mention that at Santa Rosa, in the extreme north-east point of the country, we found that the inhabitants had banded themselves together in a rifle club, to protect themselves from plundering expeditions fitted out in Corrientes. In former times of revolution, the enterprising citizens of Corrientes, who enjoy a very high reputation for violent ways, were in the habit of coming down to Santa Rosa in armed bands and plundering where and whom they would. Word having come that these kindly neighbours up the river were of opinion that another favourable opportunity had arisen for exhibiting similar friendly ways, the people of Santa Rosa wisely banded themselves together and practised rifle-shooting, so that they might receive their visitors with the honours of war and not fall an easy prey to their tender mercies as in former days.

At Salto, for three months before the revolution broke out, nothing had been coming or going on the quays, and trade was at a complete standstill, the stores of the merchants had been running out, and no effort made to replenish them, for fear of a looting at no distant date. Why is it, some may ask, that in

a republican country, with an elective system of government, revolutions should occur ?
The fact is that at present, both in the
Banda Oriental and in the Argentine republics, the presidency is practically a despotism.

After a man has been president for the
utmost limit of time the constitution allows,
the practice is for him to nominate some near
relative, and to nominate is to elect, for the
Government has enormous voting influence
through the vast body of officials connected
with public works of all kinds, the army,
railways, post office, telegraphs, and customs,
and when these influences are insufficient,
elections are carried by manipulating the
ballotings. So the office of president remains
in the family circle, and the people have no
real choice. President Santos, though hated
by the aristocrats because he had sprung from
the ranks, and hated by the people because he
taxed them heavily and misused the public
money, was certainly a man of power, and had
he administered the finances with some regard
to the proportion due to himself, and punished

officials who plundered, would not have been a bad ruler for the country. But everywhere the sweets of power are attractive, and men are reluctant to descend from the presidential throne. Why is it, one cannot help asking, that republics have presidents ? Surely the logical position of a republic is that of a state without a president. Switzerland is the true ideal republic.

Within six months of the suppression of the revolution an attempt was made to assassinate General Santos. The bullet went through his cheek, and for a time his life seems to have been in danger. Before he fully recovered he resigned the presidency and left the country. General Tajes, the successful leader of the forces which crushed the revolution, has been appointed president. Many of the revolutionary leaders have been given portfolios, a general amnesty proclaimed, and a decree passed banishing Santos from the country. So that the bullet of the assassin appears to some extent to have accomplished, what an armed revolution in the field failed to effect.

CHAPTER XIV.

SALTO.

LIKE other towns and cities of the River
Plate, Salto, in its street architecture, bears
much resemblance to an Italian city. The
reason of this is that large numbers of the
working population are Italian immigrants,
who naturally build and decorate their houses
in a style similar to that which they are
acquainted with in their own country. At a
little distance from the town, the flat roofs and
the absence of chimneys cause the houses to
look like a number of large packing-cases, the
only fires required being the smokeless charcoal stoves used for cooking purposes.

In the big town of Salto, strange to say,
there is no bank. There was once a local
bank here, which, as I was told, after lending

the bulk of its deposits to friends of the
directors, closed its doors with as much grace
as the circumstances would admit. Owing to
there being no bank or exchange office when
I was there, I found it impossible to cash a
Bank of England note. The landlord of the
hotel handed it round to his friends, who
smelt it in turn, as if they could test its value
in that manner. They had evidently never
seen the like before, and with many apologies
it was returned to me. Numbers of the
people here must have large sums of money
in their houses, and how they can sleep in
comfort in their beds may seem to some
surprising. It may help to explain matters
when I say that common larceny is practically
unknown. They will do you in a bargain,
but will not steal your goods. Bolts and
bars may be dispensed with, save in cases of
riotous disturbance. The fact is that anything like a professional criminal class is non-
existent. Everyone has employment, and if
the less well-to-do cannot be called the independent rich, they certainly can be called

the independent poor, and are quite above
stealing.

Owing to the rapidity with which burial
follows death throughout South America,
there is no time to make coffins between the
time of death and the time of burial. Coffins
accordingly have to be kept in stock ready
made, of all sizes. There are shops which
contain coffins, and coffins only, suited to all
tastes and means. In the
main street of Salto there is
a large coffin shop, from the
outside of which depends a
huge signboard with a life-
size coffin depicted on it, as
here appears. One evening,
while we were at Salto, the
proprietor had quite a big

SIGNBOARD.

show, and must have spent a quantity of
dollars in dressing out mutes in different
attractive styles. One specimen of funeral
was labelled 'à la Jerusalem,' but I don't
know whether it was quite correct. We supposed that the recent battle led to this

specially grand display of various styles of becoming burial.

From Salto I visited the neighbouring saladero, about two miles down the river. The ingenious arrangements for converting an ox in an incredibly short space of time into preserved meat, hermetically sealed in neatly labelled tins, are well known. Only the prime parts of the meat are tinned, the coarser portions being merely sun-dried. The sun-dried or jerked beef, called in the country 'chaca,' is exported in large quantities to Brazil, where it is consumed by the native labouring class. During the recent visitation of cholera (January–February, 1887), many of the saladeros of the Banda Oriental had to cease working, owing to Brazil closing her frontier against everything coming from the Banda Oriental, most of the jerked beef being exported to Brazil. The great importance of the jerked beef trade may be gathered from the following figures. In 1883 the export of meat products from the Banda Oriental was as follows: Of extract of meat, 1,000,000 lbs. ; of preserved meat, 3,300,000 lbs. ; of chaca (sun-dried meat), 76,700,000 lbs.

Before the trade in preserved meat sprang up, cattle were valuable solely for their hides, and every effort was directed to breeding cattle all hide and no meat. But the preserved-meat factories have already made a change in this, and if the frozen-meat trade should become important, the aim of the cattle breeders will be directed to producing animals all meat and no hide. The frozen-meat trade seems likely to be of slow growth, for frozen meat does not appear to be so palatable or so easily digested as fresh meat. We had some experience of this on our voyage out and home. Going out we were fed entirely upon frozen meat, and on the voyage home we were fed upon fresh meat. Although the fresh meat was the meat of animals in far from good condition, owing to the discomforts of the voyage, the fresh-killed meat was certainly more palatable and digestible than the prime but frozen joints we had on the voyage out.

The average value of cattle in the Plate

(taking one with another) is 25s., and the average value of sheep is 3s. 3d. Cattle for the butcher fetch about 40s. to 50s. each and sheep 5s. I asked an estanciero what was the lowest price at which it would pay him to sell wool, and his reply was $5\frac{1}{2}d$. per lb. One cannot be twenty-four hours in a private house in the Banda Oriental or in the Argentine Republic without being struck by the abundant table kept. It 'snoweth in the house' of meats. Three or four persons sitting down to breakfast have set before them as many dishes of meat of various kinds. This will happen again at lunch and again at dinner. At first it seems extravagant to the last degree, but when one comes to realise that prime meat is 2d. per lb. and that good legs of mutton can be got for 9d. a-piece, it gradually dawns upon one that the meat bill after all will not be a very tremendous one. Eggs and butter, however, are not cheaper than in England. The climate does not suit cocks and hens very well, and there is much trouble with the butter. In the English houses one

has all that one can desire to eat, but the
tables of the native estancieros lack many
things. They groan with meats, but with
meats only. Vegetables, fruits, milk, tea, and
butter are absent. Though extremely well-to-
do, the estancieros do not make the slightest
effort to procure either vegetables, milk, or
butter. The wonder is how they enjoy such
good health, feeding as they do so exclusively
on a meat diet. It is thought that the 'maté'
which they so freely consume supplies in some
degree the lack of other vegetable diet. Maté,
or Jesuit tea as it is sometimes called, is a
true tea. It consists of the leaves of a small
shrub chopped rather fine, and the tea-pot is
a gourd. The maté is first put in, then some
lumps of sugar are embedded in the maté,
and, lastly, the hot water is poured in; then
the bombelia (which has a long hollow stem,
the spoon-shaped bowl being perforated as
shown in the sketch) is inserted into the
bowl, and very slowly, just drop by drop, the
tea is sucked through. Men and women may
be seen in Brazil and the Plate absorbing

maté all day long, with the deliberation
of a smoker enjoying his pipe. It is good
manners to hand one's maté bowl round, like
a snuff-box, for all the company to imbibe it
in turn. When so offered, it must not be
refused, no matter who had the last suck.
Maté in taste is not unlike green tea with a
touch of senna. Although the best coffee is
produced in abundance in Brazil, the natives

MATÉ BOWLS AND BOMBELIA.

greatly prefer maté, so that it must possess
real merits for those who have acquired a taste
for it.

In spring the uplands about Salto are
carpeted with crimson verbena, of the most
brilliant colour. The flora in the Plate
district does not seem to be very varied.
About Salto we found several varieties of

sorrels much like our English wood-sorrel, but with bulbous roots, the blossoms varying from white and pale lilac to dark pink and shades of yellow ; a pretty little blue nemophila, and a curious little trefoil related apparently to the same family as the English lotus, on each stalk of which, growing bolt upright, and looking like a soldier standing at attention, was a solitary yellow blossom. None of these exceeded two inches in height.

At Salto there are numbers of curious little dogs like black-and-tan terriers, only without one scrap of hair on them, save white eyebrows and whiskers, which look very strange in contrast to their smooth black shiny skins. This absence of hair seems like a provision of nature for their comfort against their too numerous foes.

Piled alongside the railway at Salto, awaiting transport to Europe, we saw an immense heap of rough agates, looking like large flints. These are exported to Germany and manufactured into the innumerable little pebble boxes, letter-weights, and other trifles one meets with at seaside bric-à-brac stalls. At Salto a few are sold, reimported from Europe, but they are very dear, being subject to an import duty of 50 per cent.

Under the rule of General Santos there was great dishonesty in the collection of the customs duties. The irregularities were popularly attributed to the President, and every dollar that failed to reach the public treasury was supposed to have gone into his pockets. How far this was from being the case may be gathered from a remark made by the collector of customs at Salto when we were there, who, having expressed an eager desire to get promoted to Monte Video, added in the most candid way, 'If I was only at Monte Video for eighteen months, I could live at ease for the rest of my days.' Since General Tajes has become President there has been a great change for the better in the customs administration of the Banda Oriental, and the new brooms who have been set to work exhibit such a desire for clean sweeping, that merchants complain of their excessive probity and love of red-tape. In a country with extensive and remote frontiers such as Brazil, it is perhaps impossible to answer for the integrity of all the custom-house officials. The people who bribe them, however, are neither the producers nor consumers, but the forwarding agents. An estanciero sends down, say, 3,000 hides from some frontier town on the Uruguay River to Monte Video. When these hides arrive in the Banda Oriental territory, the permit is found to be made out for 1,500 only, the forwarding agents and the custom-house officials having passed out 3,000 hides as 1,500, and divided the duty upon the remaining 1,500 between them. Such transactions, though profitable to those who take part in them, bring no advantage to the Brazilian farmer.

CHAPTER XV.

ACROSS THE PLAINS.

ONE of the results of the disturbances caused
by the revolutionary movement was an
almost total cessation of passenger traffic
upon the North Western of Uruguay line.
So few people were moving about, that for a
little while after the outbreak of hostilities,
one train only each way every other day was
found to be amply sufficient for the traffic.
As there was no train running on the day
we wanted to make a start for the Cuareim
River, it became necessary for us to have a
'special.' We left Salto at 7 o'clock A.M.,
and, after stopping at several stations to look
at the line, we arrived at Isla de Cabellos
(then the terminus of the line) at 11 o'clock
A.M. We passed a considerable encampment

of soldiers near the Arapey bridge, the last
battalions of the force that was posted here to
prevent the apprehended landing of the revolutionists at this point of the river.

From Isla de Cabellos four of us, with a
peon who acted as our body servant, started
on horseback for the Cuareim River just
beyond Santa Rosa. We rode from noon till
sunset (6.30), at a steady pace, varying the
amble by cantering now and again, which
was a great relief to me, unaccustomed as I
was to the motion of the Uruguayan horses.
The endless rolling downs over which we
rode appeared to be very beautiful of their
kind, splendid downlands rolling on in great
billows league after league, and bearing a
marked resemblance to our own Dorset downs
at home, only cast in a rather larger mould,
the finest pasture land simply waiting for
men to come and run up fences, and needing
absolutely nothing more to make the best of
grazing farms. Elsewhere one hears of the
toil of settlers in clearing their land, labour
which in many parts means an initial cost of

from 5*l.* to 15*l.* an acre. But on the rolling
downs of Uruguay man is called upon to do
nothing, for the land is provided ready for
him, with the best possible of permanent pas-
turage laid down for his use. No wonder
that during the last few years of great general

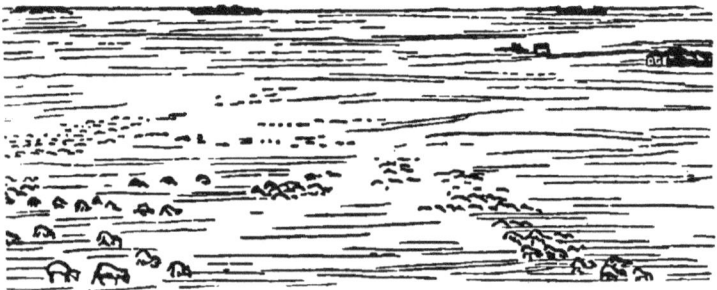

THE PLAINS.

depression, the River Plate country has come
through it almost untouched.

On these endless grassy downs there are
no trees, save just along the gullies of the
little streams, and about the estancias, which
dot the plains at intervals of about every three
miles. Though we were at an elevation of
certainly not over a thousand feet, the air was
as invigorating and delicious as on a moun-

tain-top, which may perhaps be due to its
excessive purity. The herds of cattle and the
flocks of sheep we passed seemed absolutely
countless, as we rode on hour after hour, on
the springy sward, without drawing rein for
a single gate.

We passed numbers of ostriches (rhea),
which came quite close to us, and here and

OSTRICHES.

there herds of deer. Also large numbers of a
very handsome bird, the teru-tero—a kind of
peewit—so called from its cry. It is much
disliked by sportsmen, as it possesses the soul
of a common informer, and gives notice of
their approach to other game. We saw many
fine tawny-winged vultures, some beautiful
white herons, and numbers of little owls,
which sat about on any small eminence they
could find, and blinked away in the full blaze

of the sun. We smelt the strong odour of a
skunk, but did not see him. By the side of
a marshy pool we saw some beautiful white
herons which allowed us to come close up to

WHITE HERONS.

them. We passed many of the carts of the
country drawn by long teams of oxen. The
weight these carts carry is amazing. It is
not uncommon for three, four, or five tons
to be loaded on their two great wheels, ten
to twelve feet in diameter. These carts make
very slow progress, just crawling along at
a snail's pace. The drivers camp out at
night in the open fields, and the oxen graze
where they will on the plains, no one objecting. We met great droves of cattle coming
down from Rio Grande to the saladeros of
Northern Uruguay. These also feed *en route*

without charge, but the time cannot be far
distant when the landowners will raise objections, one result of which will be an increase
of traffic on the railways.

OX CART.

We slept at night at a small ranche on the
plains, where the accommodation was rough
enough. But, rolled up in sufficient rugs on
a 'catre'—the local trestle bed—with the stars
shining brightly through the chinks in the
roof overhead, I slept soundly. Our peon slept
on the ground outside under his heavy poncho
(see p. 214), every portion of him, including
his head, tucked carefully away underneath it.
Next morning, before breakfast, we pushed on
to Santa Rosa, and later in the day went down
to the Cuareim River, which forms the northern
boundary between the Banda Oriental and
Brazil. Small by comparison with the Uruguay River, into which it runs three miles

beyond Santa Rosa, the Cuareim is yet a large
river, being about three times the width of the
Thames at Westminster Bridge. The river,
however, is very shallow during most of the
year, and even when in full flood the water
does not come down with a rush, being
mainly flood water from the Uruguay River.
The padre of Santa Rosa told us he remembered the Cuareim River entirely drying up,
and that the people of Santa Rosa went out
and had a feast in the bed of the stream,
which is of solid rock, to celebrate the event.
I have never seen more beautifully coloured
crystal pebbles than those which lie in multi-
tudes along the bed of the Cuareim River. I
filled my pockets with as many as a due
regard for the feelings of my horse would
allow me to carry.

Brazil has no harbour worthy of the name
south of Santos. The result of this is that
the southern provinces of Brazil have no sea-
outlet except by the Uruguay River. Consequently the trade carried on by the southern
provinces with the outside world goes by

way of the Uruguay River, and not through Brazilian ports.

The Uruguay River is generally navigable for 200 miles, and at times for 400 miles, above Santa Rosa. From Santa Rosa to Salto the river for purposes of navigation is useless. All transit of traffic over this portion of it has to go by land, except at times of unusual flood, which generally occurs in the months of August and September, when a certain amount of down traffic is possible. The river falls about a hundred and fifty feet in the hundred miles between Santa Rosa and Salto, and the numerous boulders and rapids practically stop navigation between these towns. To provide for this traffic, the North Western of Uruguay Railway has been built on the Banda Oriental side, and the East Argentine Railway on the Argentine side. The bulk of the traffic will probably before long go by the Banda Oriental line—which, though the first commenced, has been the last finished of these two lines— as nine out of every ten tons of goods that are sent up the Uruguay into South Brazil

to which dwellers in the Argentine Republic
are subject, and this is a decided disadvan-
tage to any country which looks to attracting
new settlers ; for, other things being equal,
newcomers prefer the country where taxation is least onerous. The prospect, however,
of the Banda Oriental joining the Argentine
Republic is remote, for Brazil would raise the
strongest objections, and by the terms of her
guarantee England would be bound to support Brazil.

Precisely the same holds good in reference
to any reunion between the Banda Oriental
and Brazil, but this is an event which would
not be the least likely to occur as long as
Brazil remains as she is now. There is, however, a third alternative which might possibly
arise. It is far from unlikely that, before many
years are over, Brazil will break up into two,
or more, separate countries. There are several
causes tending in this direction : the antago-
nism which exists between the comparatively
energetic dwellers in South Brazil, and the
sleepy, stationary, mixed races of tropical

Brazil : the strong preference for a republican form of government which prevails in the southern provinces : and the unwieldy size of the country and its geographical configuration, which from want of rivers to draw the people together does not foster union. All these tend to render it by no means improbable that the southern provinces of Brazil will set up an independent existence, and then, after a temporary separate existence, they may very naturally enter into a union with the Banda Oriental.

CHAPTER XVI.

THE LAND OF TONGUES.

AFTER leaving Salto, we paid a visit to Concordia on the opposite bank of the river, in the
province of Entre Rios, in the Argentine Republic. Thence we dropped down the river to
Paysandù, passing on our way, a little above
Paysandù, the dangerous Corralitos reef, so
named from the rocks lying in a circle in the
bed of the river. We next passed the entrance
to the Arroyo Mala, in the neighbourhood
of which is Las Delicias and several other fine
estancias, and a little later the bold bluff of Mesa
de Artigas, so called because in the war of independence (1814) General Artigas rolled his
prisoners of war, sewn up in ox-hides, down
the cliff side into the river below.

Paysandù (Pay, father ; Sandù, name of

a Jesuit priest), the second city in the Banda Oriental, is a large thriving place. Its importance is mainly due to its being, though some way up the river, a fairly good port for seagoing ships, as vessels of from 500 to 600 tons burden can discharge here, while at Salto there is not depth of water for ships of more than from 200 to 300 tons. Paysandù stands

LAS DELICIAS.

back from the river about a mile, situated on a hill looking down on the port, with which it is connected by a tramway. The country round is well wooded and the lands very fertile, and in the streets of the town there are many trees, which give it a very attractive appearance.

As yet no railway has come to Paysandù.

Before long the Midland Railway of Uruguay
will connect Paysandù with Salto towards the
west, and, by effecting a junction with the
Central Uruguay Railway at Paso de los
Toros (Bull-Ford), will connect Paysandù
with Monte Video towards the east. It is a
kind of accepted belief that a railway cannot
answer along the course of a navigable river.
It might be so if great rivers were always upon
their good behaviour ; but unfortunately they
are not, and when one considers what discomforts wet windy days entail upon travellers on
a river at least half a mile wide, it is not
difficult to realise the determined preference
exhibited for travelling by rail when there is
the opportunity of doing so. The steamer
drops anchor 100 yards from the shore, a
small boat comes off, and one has, at great dis-
advantage, to drive a hurried bargain with the
boatman. It rains pitilessly, one's poor little
traps and belongings get thoroughly saturated
and knocked about, and one finds oneself de-
posited, as likely as not, in a sea of mud, which
must be traversed somehow for fifty yards or

more, before the tram-car or a carriage can be
reached. This is what disembarkation really
means on a giant river, and at times the
miseries of it can hardly be exaggerated. For
goods traffic there are all the vexations connected with the custom-houses, for not a bale
of goods can be shipped for transit by river,
even from one town to another in the same
province, without as much investigation as if
it were going to a foreign country. When
duties are levied upon exports as well as upon
imports, transit by river involves trouble both
when shipping and when landing the cargo.

The portion of the Midland Railway which
is about to be made between Salto and Paysandù will be about eighty-five miles in
length. The country is precisely similar to
that through which the North Western of
Uruguay Railway runs, consisting of fenced-
in cattle farms on undulating grassy plains, in
part with deep rich soil, but mostly with a
friable rock just below the surface. The land
in this part of the country, and also in the
province of Salto, looks as if it might prove to

be specially suitable for the growth of the
vine. In a few places attempts in this direction have been made, and near Salto I saw a
vineyard which looked most promising. Olives
and oranges do well in the gardens, but no
serious effort has been made to cultivate them
for profit.

We visited Maccoll's ox-tongue preserving
establishment at Paysandù, the products of
which are so well known on English breakfast
tables. I was surprised to find how small a
place it was, and then I discovered that of the
500,000 tongues Maccoll supplies to his customers yearly, only a tenth part (50,000) are
cured and tinned at Paysandù. This is only
what one would expect when one comes to re-
flect, for where the cattle are slaughtered there
must the tongues be preserved. They cannot
be carried about in a hot sub-tropical climate
before they are tinned, especially as it is in
summer that the saladeros work, when the
cattle are in prime condition after feeding on
the spring herbage. I was rather amused one
day in London, in the spring of 1887, to be

told, as an alarming piece of news in connection with cholera, which had broken out in the
Banda Oriental, that Maccoll's establishment
at Paysandù had been entirely closed. I
rather surprised my informant when I remarked that even if Maccoll's establishment
at Paysandù was entirely closed, it would
only mean that the establishment which produced a tenth part of the 'Paysandù ox
tongues' was not in work.

One thing much needed at Paysandù, as
indeed everywhere in the Banda Oriental, is
improved roads. There was much rain when
we were there, and more than once it took
five horses abreast to get our light covered
van through the slough of mud. Dwellers in
the Banda Oriental are apt to complain of the
taxation they have to bear. It may be somewhat heavier than in the Argentine Republic,
yet it is difficult for an Englishman to sym-
pathise deeply with their complaints in this
respect. The indirect taxation the 'Orientals'
are subject to, chiefly in the form of duties at
the custom-house on imported manufactured

goods, is heavy, varying from 30 to 75 per
cent. But the direct taxation (in town and
country alike) is comparatively light, being
about one-half per cent. on the capital value.
On a house or other real property valued at
1,000*l.*, the annual tax is one-half per cent. on

OUR LIGHT VAN

the capital value, or 5*l.* If we assume that
the interest on 1,000*l.* may be reckoned at
the rate of five per cent., the tax is a tenth of
the assumed rent. But if we put the rate of
interest as high as eight or ten per cent.,
which is the normal rate in the country, the

local tax comes to about one-twentieth of the rent, instead of amounting to one-sixth, fifth, or even fourth of the rent, as too often happens in urban districts at home. This method of levying the tax on the capital value, and not on the letting value, is certainly a very fair one. An English mansion sells for, say, 10,000*l.* and lets for 200*l.* a year. We tax it, not on its capital value, but on its letting value. On its capital value, calculated at four per cent., it would be rated at 400*l.* a year, and should pay accordingly. The system of levying taxes on the capital value, and not on the letting value, is followed in the Argentine Republic as well as in the Banda Oriental. It exists nearer home in the Channel Islands.

In the Banda Oriental there is a fixed maximum amount for local taxes. No matter where one takes up one's abode, one knows exactly how much one is liable to be called upon to pay. On the other hand, the local body (corresponding to a local board or town council), which has the expenditure of the money, cannot render the dwellers within the area of its jurisdiction liable to pay one farthing more than the one-half per cent. on the capital value of their property. No doubt this is the reason why so many streets and roads are badly kept, gaping open every now and again as if eager to entomb one alive. Yet in spite of such drawbacks, the ratepayers must regard the fixed law of contribution as a merciful providence watching over their interests.

During recent years there has been a heavy fall in the value of live-stock in the River Plate, mainly owing to the great increase in the world's stock of sheep and cattle. This fall in values has been in a large degree made up for by the natural increase in numbers, and much more than made up for to those who own their farms, by the enormous rise that has taken place in the value of their land. Ten years ago land could be purchased freely for from 150l. to 500l. a league (ten square miles), but similar land cannot be obtained now for less than from 1,000l. to 5,000l. a league. The picked estancias on the River Uruguay

may be put down as being worth quite 5,000*l.*
a league. The cost of purchasing a league of
good land, putting up buildings and stocking
a farm, may be estimated as follows :—

	£
One league (6,660 acres) of good land . .	3,000
Three thousand sheep at 5*s.*	850
Four hundred cattle at 2*l.*	800
Estancia buildings	300
Twenty horses at 4*l.*	80
Carts and fencing	300
Three shepherd huts	90
Corrals (inclosed yards for cattle) . . .	70
	£5,490

An estancia built for 300*l.* will not be one
of a very magnificent kind, but 'it will serve.'
A friend of mine who is farming prosperously
in the Banda Oriental, after having abandoned
New Zealand in disgust, told me that in New
Zealand he purchased 800 acres from the
State, but that to clear them and bring them
into a state of cultivation cost him about 15*l.*
an acre, and he said that his was no unusual
experience. In the Banda Oriental no clearing is necessary ; nature has done everything
except put up the fences.

The Banda Oriental most wisely maintains a gold currency, while both her neighbours, Brazil and the Argentine Republic, have a forced paper currency. The evil of a forced paper currency is the constant fluctuation in value to which it is subject. Its value never remains constant, and this adds an element of great uncertainty to every contract of a running or future character which has to be met in gold. The foreign dealer who comes to buy wool or hides in the Argentine Republic has to take into consideration the possibility of fluctuation in the rate of exchange before the time of payment has arrived, which adds an unnecessary element of risk to commercial transactions. As an instance of the way in which a forced paper currency may fluctuate, I may mention that when I left Brazil for the River Plate, I took away with me Brazilian notes to the then current value of 6*l*. On my return to Brazil two months later, these notes were worth a trifle over 8*l*., the premium on gold having fallen so considerably in that short time.

South America is not altogether a bad field for governesses. They are very fairly paid and have good opportunities of marrying well. One lady told me that she had nothing but trouble with her governesses, for they no sooner came out than they got married. She said that she felt inclined to make an agreement with them that they should not leave her for at least a year after coming out, but that she was afraid they might make themselves disagreeable if under terms of this kind. Daily governesses naturally make the largest incomes, and I was told of one in Rio who was earning as much as 250*l*. a year. Some governesses, however, do not like the sort of life they have to put up with at all. One governess we met was leaving a very comfortable place because there was no church to go to on Sundays, and she felt she could not get along without it.

Before passing on to the Argentine Republic, I must say a few words concerning the horses of the Banda Oriental. They are firm, sound, and sinewy, with

capital quarters, shapely heads, and clean
legs. They work splendidly, and can do
their forty miles a day easily, with no other
feed than the natural herbage of the country.
They are mostly of a bay colour, and very
docile. In price they range from 1*l.* to 5*l.*,
anything above the last figure being a fancy
figure. Mares are never used for riding.

The natives are very fond of equipping
their horses showily. The bits, stirrups, and
spurs are huge, and very often made of silver.
The reins also are silver mounted. These
silver trappings are thought very highly of,
and often descend for generations as heir-
looms. The spurs look like horrible instru-
ments of torture, but I do not think they are
used at all savagely. As some set-off to the
heavy bits and spurs, the horses are ridden
unshod, and the firmness of tread resulting
from this is very marked. The horses are all
well saddled, and girthed under the belly
with broad string girths from about 10 to
12 inches wide. These girths give a very
firm hold to the saddle, and are cool to the

horse and a support to him in long journeys. The grip they give to the saddle is very necessary for the purpose of using the lasso, which is attached to a ring on the saddle. When lassoing a bullock, two men fling lassos simultaneously, and gallop off in different directions; the lassos come taut with a sudden jerk, flinging the bullock on the ground and trying girths, horses, and riders to the utmost. Small boys spend hours practising with the lasso at a horned skull of an ox laid on the ground. It is fortunate that horses are so cheap, as it enables everyone to ride. Workmen going to their work ride; the milkman comes to your door on horseback; the beggars would ride if there were any, but luckily there are none, save here and there a cripple incapable of bestriding a horse, who is licensed to solicit alms. The milkman makes his butter on his rounds to his customers. On either side of his saddle hang two long tin canisters full of milk, and the jog-trot of the horse converts the contents into butter as he rides along. He does not sell the milk with-

N

out the butter ; if you take butter you can
have milk, but not *vice versâ*.

When travelling any distance, especially
if time is important, several spare horses
are taken, and as one horse tires, he is un-
saddled and recovers himself by travelling
unburdened. The horses are about fourteen
and a half hands high. Their pace—they
travel about six miles an hour—is very trying
at first ; it is an amble, the rider jogging on
without rising in the saddle. The seat of the
natives is that of the warrior, with long straight
leg, riding by balance, not the bent knee of the
jockey. It occurred to me that our military
authorities might do well to mount a portion
of our light cavalry on these horses. Any
number of them can be got, which, including
transit to England, would not cost more than
from 15*l*. to 20*l*. each. The regular cavalry
of the Banda Oriental, of which we saw a
considerable number, were as well mounted
a body of troops as one would wish to see.
Their horses would look a trifle small be-
side our cavalry regiments, but they were

thoroughly fitted for their work, and indeed likely to easily wear out more heavily built horses.

In England we convey land by documents of formal shape ; in the River Plate countries they convey horses thus. In order to facilitate the documentary identification of horses every horse has a conspicuous mark branded on his hind quarters. These marks are carefully described in the government documents of title which all owners of horses possess, and without which no transfer of a horse is valid.

CHAPTER XVII.

BUENOS AYRES AND LA PLATA.

BUENOS AYRES, with a population of some three hundred and twenty-five thousand, lies along the southern bank of the River Plate. The river is so wide at this point that the opposite shore cannot be seen, and indeed, as far as appearances go, the city might be situated on the open sea. Like Monte Video, the city is well placed with regard to effect, and presents a grand appearance when approached by water. Unfortunately for Buenos Ayres, the expanse of water lying before it is so shallow that the great ocean-going vessels have to lie nine miles out, unless they care to risk coming up a narrow buoyed channel to the Boca.

Landing at Buenos Ayres from an ocean-going steamer accordingly involves a long journey by boat, and, as even the boats draw too much water to get to shore, high two-wheeled carts are driven into the water, until the water just covers the horses' backs, their heads alone being above water, and into these carts the passengers and their baggage are transferred.

Buenos Ayres will bear comparison, as far as buildings go, with European cities. Throughout the city palatial buildings are rapidly taking the place of moderate-sized houses, the larger and more imposing structures being already sufficiently numerous to give tone to the city. Admirable tramways run throughout the city and far into the suburbs. Buenos Ayres, like most South American cities, is laid out upon the chess-board plan. If it were not for the tramways, the roads would be found most irksome to get about, the unevenness of the metalling being simply astounding to a European. Ruts and hollows in which one could lie down and disappear abound. Several of the roads have never been metalled, and are still mere earthen tracks. In dry weather they are inches deep in dust, and when heavy rain comes on, they are a deep sea of liquid mud. Until one has seen the extraordinary way in which these earthen roads convert themselves into absolute bogs, one cannot fully appreciate how realistic is the story of the man who, picking his way along one of these mudways, saw a hat apparently floating on the surface. He kicked it with his foot, and was surprised to hear a gruff voice from underneath say,

' Leave my hat alone.'

' Who are you ? '

' Who am I ? Why, I'm the conductor on the top of an omnibus.'

One cannot expect everything to come quite straight all at once, especially when there is a limit to the rates local authorities may levy, but such little inconveniences will doubtless be righted in time.

A complete system of main drains has been constructed in Buenos Ayres. The completion of the new sewers was celebrated by a series of banquets held inside them. The authorities, however, appear to be in no hurry to complete the drainage scheme by connecting the houses with drains, and, until this is done, it is difficult to see how the drains can be of much service.

The Argentine Republic, like the United States, has a double system of government, national (or federal) and provincial. The rights of the respective governments to some extent overlap, and sometimes a conflict of jurisdictions arises. Such a conflict arose in connection with the drainage of Buenos Ayres. The sewers were built by the national government, which has its seat at Buenos Ayres.

In the course of making the sewers the authorities had to expropriate certain lands belonging to an Englishman, but before paying him for his land they sent the contractors to take possession. He refused to give up possession until he had received payment for his land, and he called in the aid of the police of the province of Buenos Ayres to protect him against the contractors. The national government replied by sending sol-

diers to oust the police of the provincial
government. A somewhat curious *impasse*.
The Plaza Victoria at Buenos Ayres
extends over eight acres, and is surrounded
by many effective buildings—the Cathedral,
Bishop's Palace, Government House, Opera
House, Post Office, and Custom House.
Buenos Ayres has about a dozen plazas of
from eight to twelve acres in size. The
largest is the Plaza Constitucion (16 acres),
formerly the great wool market, and now
chiefly remarkable for being fronted on one
side by the terminal station of the Great
Southern of Buenos Ayres Railway.

This station would probably astonish some
of the shareholders if they saw it. Its marble
halls and staircases, with magnificent lions
couchant, are laid out on truly magnificent
lines. It would put Euston or Paddington
quite into the shade. I went over the station
barracas (stores) for wool, hides, grain, etc.,
and they seemed to be excellently arranged.
Complaints are sometimes made, and perhaps
not without reason, about the free railway

passes given to strangers visiting the country by the officials of English railway companies in the Argentine Republic. When I was in Buenos Ayres, two rich young Englishmen, possessing more money than they well knew what to do with, were given the free use, for a month, of a saloon carriage on the Buenos Ayres Great Southern Railway. For that time they were able to go where they would, and hitch it on and off to any train, and in fact use it as a sort of movable shooting-box. On many lines the system of free passes causes grumbling amongst the residents, who, having to work hard for their living, see well-to-do strangers travelling about the country free of charge.

The Buenos Ayres Great Southern is one of the many successful lines of the Argentine Republic. Commenced in 1865, with a capital of 750,000*l.*, and 71 miles of rail, its capital has grown in a little over twenty years to 8,000,000*l.*, and its mileage to 825. It has paid an average dividend of 8⅝ per cent. to its shareholders, and has laid aside a reserve fund amounting to the respectable figure of 400,000*l*.

About one-third of the population (320,000) of Buenos Ayres are foreigners. The foreign immigrants, especially the Italians, keep in touch with each other by belonging to various friendly clubs and political societies, and occasionally these associations have made most imposing political demonstrations. As no one is entitled to a vote unless he formally takes up his citizenship, thousands of the most enterprising and thriving of the community are unrepresented in the councils of the State. It is therefore an advantage that they should be linked together in associations which can, when necessary, make their voices heard. It would be better, however, if residents of three years' standing were allowed to exercise the franchise, so that their interests and opinions might have due weight in the councils of the country, of which they form a valuable and important element. The English-speaking community in the River Plate is a very small one and chiefly confined to the upper middle class, merchants and estancieros. Of the three strands which make up the English-speaking people, the Irish take the lead in the River Plate, next rank the Scotch, and last in point of number and importance come the English proper.

It is well worth the trouble of gaining admission to the museum at Buenos Ayres. I say trouble, because we always found it shut, and only got in at last by favour. The fossil forms of antediluvian animals are very remarkable. Great, colossal, scaly armadillos, perfect in every point, yet in spite of their enormous size showing striking marks of elementary development. They seemed to say to one pathetically, ' We have not survived—how could we ? You can see for yourselves we were never properly equipped for the struggle of life.'

There is a great deal of stucco in the buildings of Buenos Ayres, but in a climate where this material is able to resist ' the tooth of time ' for years together, it is not so objectionable as in England. The prevalence of

stucco is due to the absence of building stone,
and the absence of building stone is due to
the province of Buenos Ayres, for 200 miles
from the capital, being nothing but one vast
tract of rich alluvial deposit. It is owing
to the wealth of the province in good soil,
that architecturally the city is weak. It is
really a land of brick, and of brick only, and
of brick its buildings shŏuld be built.

Both the English banks at Buenos Ayres
are housed in splendid buildings. Handsome,
airy, and admirably finished in every particular, they would be an ornament to any city.
It seemed rather strange, on going into such
stately buildings, to find the clerks doing their
work in their shirt sleeves, many of them
smoking the everlasting cigarette. No doubt
the feeling of incongruity would wear off, but
it shows how what we call the ' proprieties '
have to give way before the intense heat and
languor of a sub-tropical country.

The province of Buenos Ayres possesses a
soil almost unequalled for richness, a splendid
climate, and the advantage of being bounded

on three sides by sea or river : although
only a tenth of the whole Argentine Republic
in area, it is as large as Great Britain and
Ireland together. The Argentine national
government borrows largely in foreign markets, and the governments of most of the provinces do the same; the province of Buenos
Ayres, owing to her great natural advantages,
borrows on as good terms as the national
government.

The national and provincial governments
can each grant concessions and raise loans for
similar purposes, which is somewhat confus-
ing and misleading to the foreign lender. In
the case of railways, for example, the provincial governments can grant concessions for
making railways, or for raising loans for such
purposes, within the limits of their own terri-
tories. The national government has similar
powers extending over all the provinces.
Consequently unless the joint consent of
both is obtained, which frequently is not
done, a successful railway made under a
provincial concession may be paralleled by

another railway built under a national concession, or *vice versâ*.

To select a perfectly unoccupied site, and
to straightway erect thereon a complete range
of government buildings of every description,
—legislative chambers, law-courts, treasury,
official residences, railway stations, museums—
all on the most magnificent scale, without
any intermediate growth from smaller beginnings, is a thing unknown to us in the Old
World. Yet this is what has happened at La
Plata. Until 1880 the province of Buenos
Ayres dominated the Argentine Republic.
In wealth and population she outweighed the
other provinces, although in area they vastly
exceeded her in size. But with the growth of
the provinces the domination of Buenos Ayres
was threatened. This was too much for their
pride, and the provincial government, being
no longer able to rule, determined in 1880 to
secede from the Confederation. The provincial
leaders were eager enough for independence,
but the people were only half-hearted about it.
They were more intent upon their crops, their

business and their profits, than upon the political status of their province. The result was that after a short, hollow struggle, the revolt collapsed, and the provincial government had to take up a subordinate position.

But this was not quite all. The provincial government had hitherto enjoyed the privilege of raising troops of their own. Had it not been for this, the attempt to secede could never have been made. The national government now withdrew from the provincial government this privilege, and the provincial government were, moreover, given to understand, that there was no longer any room for them in the city of Buenos Ayres. This was the reason of the rise of La Plata. The fiat of the provincial government accordingly went forth, a site was chosen, and thirty miles from Buenos Ayres, in three years, out of the bare plain, the new capital of the province arose. Nothing could be more striking than to see, side by side, the grand new station rearing itself loftily alongside the little wooden shed which, when I was there, was still doing

duty until the new station should be finished.
The contrast was startling between the palatial station—far more beautiful to look upon
than most of our costly modern classic buildings in Parliament Street—and the little hut
beneath it, looking hardly larger than a good-
sized packing case. As the whole of the
government business of the province, legislative and executive, must of necessity be trans-
acted at La Plata, there is a great coming
and going of business people, and, in addition to numerous public officials, numbers of
agents of all descriptions, find it necessary to
reside there permanently. The deputies also
must reside during the sittings, and to provide for the wants of all these people, numerous
tradespeople are drawn together. The result
is that a population of 40,000 has been called
together to form a city in the space of three
years, where before there was nothing but a
few scattered farms.

Fine buildings were rapidly approaching
completion on all sides. Into one of these,
which I found to be the new museum, I strolled

unobserved, and had a good look at numbers of excellent specimens of stuffed birds, and also at some very indifferent pictures. Of the birds, the *Polyborus thorus*—buteo (falcon) —cathartes (vulture)—and numerous members of the owl family, were especially worth seeing. When I had just completed my investigations, an official who was busy arranging cases in a remote chamber, courteously informed me that the museum was not yet opened to the public, and that I must depart.

The oven bird is common in the River Plate, and is especially partial to a wooden telegraph-post as a building site. In the neighbourhood of Ensenada nearly every telegraph-post has its nest, many of the posts carrying two of these domiciles. The hum of the wires doubtless proves a soothing lullaby to the inmates. The nest, which is about the size of a man's head, is in shape somewhat akin to a wren's nest, but rounder, and is composed of mud and straw, like that of an English house-martin. The opening, which is in front, is large and circular, and·

within there is a screen right across the
entrance, which makes a hall to the real nest
beyond, no doubt to keep the draught out.
Owing to the cost of wooden telegraph-posts,
old rails are now much used for the purpose
of carrying the wires. The oven bird has not
as yet taken to the iron telegraph-posts.

La Plata is lighted by electricity, and the
lamp-posts have been very cleverly utilised
for the double duty of carrying lamps and
telegraph wires. I see no reason why this
excellent plan should not be generally adopted.
Passing out of La Plata towards Ensenada,
the 'bond' goes under a kind of 'Temple
Bar' archway, of a decidedly effective character, next through a thick belt of well-
grown eucalyptus trees, and then down a
gentle descent about three miles to the port of
Ensenada. Here the provincial government
has expropriated an immense area, and built
quays, docks, and barracas, sufficient for a
very large trade. Ensenada has a double advantage over Buenos Ayres as a port, in that
ships can reach Ensenada by a buoyed channel

something under four miles, instead of nine
miles, in length, and that owing to the provincial government hving expropriated the
whole of the land there, for the harbour and
quays, the dues are much less, and the rent
of the barracas lower, than at Buenos Ayres.
Buenos Ayres, however, possesses the traffic
which Ensenada hopes to get, and whether
Ensenada will be able to divert it, or any
substantial portion of it, can only be determined by the lapse of time.

Ensenada is a very long straggly place,
and on the rainy afternoon I was there presented a most dismal appearance.   The state
of the road for a mile from where the tram
put me down was one continuous quagmire
of the most awful character.   I gave myself
up for lost more than once, and fully expected
to be dug out in some remote geological period
—a curious and interesting fossil.

CHAPTER XVIII.

THE CAMP.

THERE is plenty of shooting to be had in the
' Camp,' as the country is called in the province
of Buenos Ayres. Swan, goose, flamingo,
duck, grebe, water-hen, snipe, partridge, deer,
ostrich, skunk, hare, and guanaco (a sort
of deer) make up a very good bag. The
partridge is rather larger than our English
bird, but disappointing when cooked, the
flesh being white and rather tasteless. Those
who want better sport than a comparatively
settled country can afford, will take the comfortable river steamers to the Grand Chaco
or Paraguay, where they will meet with game
in abundance of all kinds.

Much of the country about Buenos Ayres is
well cultivated. A kind of clover called 'alfalfa'

grows with prodigious rapidity. We saw a
field of it growing with the utmost luxuri-
ance, from which five crops had been cut
within the preceding twelve months. I was
struck by seeing whole fields of tomatoes
trained on sticks like peas, and bearing most
abundantly. The land is nearly all fenced
in with fences made of iron wire run on
nandubay posts. Nandubay is an extremely
hard wood, iron-like in texture. It is so
hard that the posts are not squared into
formal shape, and the effect is rather pleasing.
It is a kind of acacia, of small growth, and
resists decay for a hundred years. Vast
quantities of nandubay posts have been cut
in Entre Rios and Corrientes. It is greatly
in request for railway-sleepers, but is now
getting very scarce.

Riding about the country, one often sees
for long distances together, innumerable ab-
surd little owls (*Athene cunicularia*), sitting
on every post. Daylight does not seem to
inconvenience them as it does their English
cousins. They appear very friendly, and will

let one come almost near enough to touch them. They gaze at one with much interest : their heads only moving and almost imperceptibly. As they never take their eyes off one, and never move their bodies in order to get a better view of one, their heads only travelling round while their bodies remain immovable, one has only to walk round one of them in order to twist its neck.

The roads in the Camp are mere tracks, and very decidedly rough for driving over to those who are not used to them ; for unless one's trap is built so that the wheels fit into the ruts made by the bullock waggons, one travels with one wheel in a rut and the other often elevated a foot up, making an upset a most likely occurrence. Roads cannot be said to exist except in the immediate neighbourhood of the big cities in the Argentine Republic. This is equally true of the Banda Oriental. They are mere tracks, which in bad weather become impassable. Bridges, metalled roads, and road drainage, are as yet non-existent. In Uruguay there is a good supply of materials for making roads, but over an immense area of Buenos Ayres, and in many other parts, there are no road-making materials of any kind to be obtained. The result is that it is actually cheaper in such places to make railways than roads. Good railways can be made and coached for about 5,000*l.* a mile. Hence the efforts made, and wisely made, by the Argentine Republic to extend its railway system.

As long as there are neither roads nor railways the country suffers, like the human body, from numerous ills arising from want of proper circulation. In a roadless land agriculture cannot be profitably carried on ; cattle and sheep, which can carry themselves to market, alone are profitable : and there are limits even to their value. Owing to railway companies being so essential to the welfare of the country, they are not kept so much at arms-length as they are with us at home. It is quite a normal state of things to have level crossings in the busiest cities, trains not being expected to get out of every one's way.

Engine-drivers, however, are held responsible if they run over anyone; this is somewhat hard upon them, for as a rule they are not to blame.

One day when leaving Buenos Ayres by train, we suddenly experienced a jerking and jolting, and the train was abruptly brought to a full-stop; the guard announced that we had knocked over a cart and had killed both horse and driver. In spite of the line being in full sight for some way, and also regardless of the engine-driver's warning whistle, the driver of the cart had kept calmly on his way, crossing the line under the nose of the engine, the natural result of which was that the cart was smashed up and the horse killed, while the driver fortunately escaped with a few bruises. A petition was at once got up and signed by all the passengers, to testify that in their opinion it was no fault of the engine-driver; it being his only chance of avoiding imprisonment for reckless driving. In spite of this happening close to Buenos Ayres, it seemed to be no one's business to remove the dead

carcass of the horse, and for many days
afterwards, we saw the animal's remains by
the side of the line, stripped of its skin.

It is quite a common occurrence for a train
to run into a herd of cattle, especially in
winter time, when the trains often have to be
stopped, and all the passengers turned out to
assist in clearing the cattle off the line, hauling
them off by their tails, legs, and horns. When
locomotives first appeared upon the plains the
ostriches were greatly astonished at them, and
not being at all inclined to welcome such
strange beasts, whole flocks of them would
run full-tilt at the offending intruders. They
have now gained wisdom by experience.

Eucalyptus trees planted either in long
single rows, or in larger masses arranged
with the utmost rectilineal accuracy, are very
common in the province of Buenos Ayres.
The native trees, which were never numerous,
have been felled for rafters, beams, and fire-
wood ; all are gone save the ombù, which is
useless for even the last of these purposes, its
wood being of so spongy a texture that it is

scarcely firmer than a cabbage-stump. It is
fortunate that the ombù has escaped the axe,
for, unlike the formal eucalyptus, it is a beautiful tree, and at a little distance looks not
unlike an English oak.

Owing to the country about Buenos Ayres
being almost a dead level, the scenery is extremely dull. The result is that the men of
business who keep country houses naturally
prefer to have them along the riverside, as
being the only really beautiful part of the
country within reach. Wharves, barracas,
docks, and quays, with all their concomitants,
monopolise the riverside eastwards of the city.
It follows that only along the river westwards,
is there any place for a fashionable quarter,
and here along this bit of river-coast, for
some twenty miles, there are great numbers
of country residences, belonging to the wealthy
people of Buenos Ayres. Every morning and
evening crowds of busy men travel to and fro
by the Buenos Ayres Northern Railway, which
serves this stretch of country. On this line,
four miles from Buenos Ayres, is Palermo.

Here on several days in the week a very good band plays, and all the rank, fashion, and beauty of the neighbourhood meet together, to see and to be seen. The grounds, covering some 840 acres, are beautifully laid out. In the park of Palermo is a small zoological

PALERMO PARK.

garden, restricted almost entirely to the Argentine fauna. In the centre of the park is a grand avenue of palms. These palms are some sort of date-palm, the blossom of which is very pretty, resembling a gigantic spike of creamy spirea. The fruit is of a pale yellow, oval shape, about the size of a big cob-nut.

Belgrano is the next station, about five miles from Buenos Ayres, a very attractive place, with many beautiful quintas (country

houses). At the end of the line, at Tigre,
some twenty miles from Buenos Ayres, a
beautifully wooded tributary river flows into
the River Plate, and here the Buenos Ayres
Rowing Club has its headquarters. The
Buenos Ayres Northern Railway has the monopoly of this valuable tract of riverside passenger traffic, yet in spite of this the ordinary
shares of the railway are below par. It is a
line which might have been made and coached
for 6,000*l.* a mile ; 10,000*l.* a mile would be
a handsome figure for a double line of rails.
At present it is for part of the way still a
single line, and yet the capital expenditure of
the company stands at 22,000*l.* a mile. The
tèrminal station in Buenos Ayres is a very
poor one, and I heard many complaints of the
way the railway fails to meet the wants of
the public. It seems strange that, with such
advantages in the way of position and traffic,
the railway should not have been a more profitable one to the shareholders.

CHAPTER XIX.

ALONG THE PARANÁ.

ROSARIO, though not the capital, is the largest
city in the province of Santa Fé. It is the
Liverpool, or perhaps, considering its rapid
growth, it might be more aptly termed the
Winnipeg of the Argentine Republic. Many
of its streets are still mere tracks of dust or
mud, according to the season, but the authorities are making fair headway, and considering
that their forerunners of a generation ago, and
even less, were the owl, the hawk, and the
wild horse, none of them specially given to
city improvements, there is not much to fairly
complain about.

In 1854 Rosario was little more than a big
village, with a population of 4,300. It has
now a population of more than 50,000, and the

tonnage of the goods traffic at the port has
risen since that date, from 8,000 to 750,000
tons. What makes Rosario so important a
place is, its being the furthest point on the
Paraná, to which large ships can come. It is,
in fact, the seaport for the large and wealthy
province of Cordova, and for the provinces
which lie further up country—Tucuman,
Salta, and Jujuy.

The important province of Cordova, which
lies to the westward of Santa Fé, entirely shut
off from river communication, save by way
of Rosario, is the second province in the
Argentine Republic, with a population of
350,000. As an instance of the enormous
rates of interest that are paid in these countries,
it may be mentioned that as recently as 1880
the wealthy province of Cordova was paying
the Bank of Cordova 18 per cent. for an
advance.

The province of Santa Fé is second only
to that of Buenos Ayres, in point of natural
advantages. The waterway along the Paraná
brings it into direct contact with the outer

world, while the country itself is bountifully favoured both as to soil and climate. It is subject neither to droughts nor floods. It is particularly favourable to the growth of wheat, and enormously heavy crops are gathered from half the quantity sown per acre, that we are accustomed to sow in England.

As far as my experience goes, hotels either omit to provide mosquito curtains altogether, or provide such as offer no effectual resistance to the mosquito. Satisfactory mosquito curtains are luxuries only met with in private houses. So detestable do these little brutes make themselves, and so merciless are they, that I think it well to mention an easy way of destroying them by a method not generally known, if one may judge from the number of bedrooms one comes across, in which the walls are blotched all over with the dead bodies of the slain, recording many a protracted hour of midnight torture. The common way to destroy a mosquito is to bludgeon it to death with a towel or a slipper. Provided the mosquito does not escape the blow, this is all very well, but they have an irritating way of eluding one. The only sure weapon is a candle, the flame of which should be held about an inch off the wall, and four inches above the mosquito, as he sits perched airing his hind legs on the wall; then slowly lower the flame down upon the enemy, and when it reaches him, he will give a splutter, and fall dead into the hot grease. Mosquitoes seem to be spellbound by a candle flame, and by resort to this method of destruction, a room may be converted in a few minutes, from a veritable inferno into a place of rest.

Only those who, when intensely weary, have suffered from the slow torture of repeated attacks from ravenous mosquitos, can fully appreciate the feelings of the Irishman who, after a conflict with mosquitos, seeing a firefly flitting round his chamber, in his despair groaned out, 'Och, Mike, here's one of thim beggars a-come to look for us with a lanthorn.'

The train by which I left Rosario started at ten o'clock, and by 12.30 we should, in the ordinary course of things, have reached a station where we might havê had the late breakfast of the country. I had debated with myself when I got up whether I would have an English breakfast before starting, or merely a roll and coffee, and trust to my luck at déjeuner at 12.30. I decided in favour of a substantial breakfast, and luckily so, for just beyond San Nicholas, we found that a train had gone off the rails and ploughed up the line for a considerable distance. As it is a single line of rails there was nothing to be done but to unload everything from our train ; carry all the luggage about half a mile along the line ; and then reload it on another train, which had been sent to pick us up. About five hours were consumed in this fairly simple proceeding. No doubt the excessive delay arose owing to the line being scarcely in proper working order, the part we were then on, having only been opened for through traffic from Buenos Ayres to Rosario, on the previous Sunday. I believe every passenger excepting myself—and the train was full—started with the intention of

P

breakfasting at 12.30. To a slight extent the hunger of the passengers 'was satisfied by a meagre supply of biscuits from the liquor bar attached to the train, and by a hatful of raw eggs procured by the barman in a raid he made upon a neighbouring estancia, which he doled out at famine prices. It was past six in the evening before the dejected and hungry passengers reached a station where any food could be obtained.

When we were at Salto we visited Concordia in the province of Entre Rios (between rivers). It is a fair-sized town and of some importance, being the terminus of the East Argentine Railway. This railway (like the North Western of Uruguay) has been built to carry the traffic over the hundred miles of country which the Uruguay river, owing to rapids, does not serve. The East Argentine line was finished in 1876, and has obtained a good deal of the traffic coming from Rio Grande and South Brazil. The line is more expensively managed than the North Western of Uruguay, and has had to depend mainly upon the Government guarantee for its dividends. Before many years have passed, the railway will, in all probability, be prolonged into Corrientes and Missiones, and thus become an important link in the highway to Paraguay. No doubt, the advent of a railway will have a sobering influence upon the somewhat lawless inhabitants of Corrientes. Missiones, which is an old Jesuit settlement further up the river, is, from all accounts, a province of extreme fertility.

For ill-treatment of goods by Custom House officials, I must give the palm to those at Concordia. I saw a large wooden case marked 'fragile' slid out of the lighter on to the shore, and then tilted over and let down with a bang on its side some fifteen to twenty times in succession. By the time it reached the cart which was to remove it to the barraca, it was loosened in all its joints, and had assumed a rhomboidal instead of rectangular shape.

Entre Rios is rather larger than Ireland, with a population not greater than that of many English counties (200,000). In general character it is very similar to the Banda Oriental, and enjoys a splendid climate. It lies wedged in between the two giant rivers, the Paraná and Uruguay, which from their width operate as barriers to communication between the province and the outer world. This, no doubt, has kept the province back, although it lies almost within hail of Buenos Ayres. But the population, though not numerous, is extremely well-to-do, and there can be little doubt that Entre Rios has a very fine future before it.

CHAPTER XX.

THE GAUCHO.

THE gauchos (native peasants) of the Argentine appear to have neither religion nor any care for ceremonies and festivals. If it were not for the forms of the oaths and curses they use, it would be impossible to know that one was in a Christian land. In this respect they differ from the gauchos of the Banda Oriental, who are very particular about the due observance of Church functions and festivals. There are not many Indians in the settled parts of the Argentine Republic. The few that may be met with appear to have no religion, and seem to be singularly free from all forms of superstition, save one which they hold to very strongly, that of objecting to being sketched or photographed. The ground of their repugnance is the belief that those whose portraits are taken die young. The gauchos of the Banda Oriental are an excellent type of peasant. They are somewhat under the medium size (about 5 ft. 6 in. to 5 ft. 8 in. in stature), physically sound and well knit together, and as servants generally are trustworthy. The general appearance of a Uruguayan gaucho mounted on his little horse —he is so constantly in the saddle, that horse and rider are well-nigh inseparable —is not unlike that of

A GAUCHO.

a Bedouin Arab, if a black slouch hat is substituted for the turban. The swarthy gaucho neither digs nor delves, but he can ride from dawn to sundown, can throw the lasso with unerring aim, and can use his butcher's knife with dexterity and dispatch (see p. 135). The poncho, which is the distinguishing feature of his dress, is an oblong fringed shawl (about two yards long by one yard wide), generally of a dun colour patterned in white, having a slit in the middle endways, through which the head is inserted. Occasionally a circular poncho is worn of a dark blue cloth lined with

BIT, STIRRUP, AND SPUR.

red. Round the neck is tied a bright coloured silk scarf, and about the waist a bright coloured belt, in which are often lodged knives and pistols. The trousers (chiripa)—of sober colour—are somewhat of Turkish cut, large, loose, and baggy, the ends being tucked into the tops of the heavy boots. The boots are rendered conspicuous by enormous silver spurs, with rowels two to three inches in diameter. A silver-mounted whip completes

the gaucho's attire, but scarcely less important are the trappings of his horse. The
saddle of richly embossed leather is adorned
by silver mountings on the pummel, while
the saddle-cloth is often of crimson cloth cut
square, the effect of which is admirable. The
stirrups of massive silver with ball-like appendages, give room for the toe only to pass
through. The heavy steel bit is silver-mounted
at the ends, and even the reins and stirrup-
leathers are mounted in silver at intervals.
Such a costume and trappings indicate a
wealthy gaucho, but as all the gauchos are not
wealthy, some have to content themselves
with plated mountings.

The gauchos are very fond of soap and
water. Water, however, in many parts becomes very scarce when rain has not fallen for
some time, especially in districts where rock
lies not far below the surface of the ground.
And when this is the case, the gauchos, in
their thirst for a bath, make raids on any
water tanks that may come in their way. I
was led to discover this in rather a curious

way. I noticed that the water tanks and reservoirs at the stations on the North Western of Uruguay Railway were mostly protected at the top by an iron grating. With some curiosity I inquired why these heavy iron gratings were placed over the tanks. The reply was that the gauchos, when these tanks were first erected with open tops, came from all the country round, with soap and towels, and washed themselves in the water, the result of which was that the boilers of the engines primed badly, and had constantly to be sent to the workshops for repairs.

The steady progress of the River Plate is largely due to the uninterrupted influx of Italian immigrants. Although the language of the country is Spanish, seventy per cent. of the immigrants are Italians, who leave their native country (though far from over-populated) to escape the scourge of conscription. Italian peasants find their boys will not settle down to work, because of the coming conscription, and when they quit service in the ranks, they return forgetful of the little they have learnt before entering the army, in too many cases physically exhausted as well as mentally deteriorated. To the agricultural classes whose children are untempered to resist the evils of a town life, the conscription is the greatest curse in life. No wonder that they emigrate in such numbers to lands where they may possess their children in peace. To capitalists this influx of Italian labour is a very mine of wealth, for it is both cheap and good. The Italian peasant, driven from Italy, where he labours for eighteen-pence a day, and lives upon the hardest fare, finds himself in luxury with three shillings a day, and prime meat at twopence a pound. These Italian peasants are preferred to all others as agricultural labourers ; they are laborious, frugal, and contented. With a little teaching in the workshops they make excellent mechanics. They need no acclimatisation, for the climate is almost precisely the same as that to which they have been accustomed. It is this unusual combination of cheap labour of excellent quality, with a rich virgin soil and fine climate,

that has enabled the River Plate to prosper
so amazingly.

Very few English people at home have .
realised as yet the magnitude and importance of the Italian migration to the River
Plate. It is estimated that in the past year
(1886) no less than 125,000 left Italy for
these new and fertile lands. For years past
the stream of emigration has been steadily
rising. It is estimated that there are now
fully 1,000,000 Italian settlers in the River
Plate district, that is, in the Argentine Republic, the Banda Oriental, and in the Brazilian
province of Rio Grande do Sul. In the province of Rio Grande in 1875, there were but
a few scattered Italian settlements, while at
the present time it is estimated that there are
no less than 75,000 Italian farmers settled in
this district, all of whom are doing extremely
well. So great is the interest taken by Italy
in those of her peasantry who have gone out
to settle in these new countries, that, although
they are in no way politically connected with
her, the Italian Government contributes to

the cost of schools established in these distant colonies, on condition that the teaching is carried on in the Italian language.

In the course of our travels I met many persons who were well acquainted with our colonies, and they all assured me that not one of them could be compared with the River Plate as to natural advantages. Their opinions appear to be confirmed by the fact, that I came across several persons who were settled in the Plate and doing well, after having tried their luck without success either in Australia, New Zealand, or the Cape. Only in the spring of this year (1887), I received the following in a letter from New Zealand. ' Till we go home. When that will be, goodness only knows, with these wretched times for poor farmers with lots of cattle, sheep, and wool to sell, and no one to buy. I hope you eat frozen mutton to give us a helping hand.' With a fruitful land, and good and cheap labour, it should be very long before bad times come to the River Plate.

In matters legal, the Argentine Republic

has not as yet earned a very high character. The administration of the law in civil causes is so unreliable, that the mercantile community generally make it a part of every important contract, that any dispute arising under it shall be settled by reference to arbitration. When the possibility of disputes arising, has to be expressly provided for in this manner, the difficulties of bargaining are increased, but at present it seems to be the only safe thing to do. I found that the 'great unpaid' of the Republic have very easy times upon the bench. At home, as everyone knows who has to do with the magisterial bench, we have three main classes of petty offenders—thieves, poachers, and drunkards, drink often taking the form of assault. The citizens of the Argentine Republic do not thieve; there are no game laws to cause them to offend: and if they take to drink, the drink itself soon handcuffs them, and puts them out of the reach of human gaolers. The magistracy of the River Plate accordingly have little enough to do.

CHAPTER XXI.

WHERE THE SHOE WILL PINCH.

IN most new countries the advantage of good
and cheap land is to some extent counter-
balanced by high wages and a high rate of
interest.   The River Plate district enjoys the
double advantage of cheap labour and cheap
land.   This enables the farmers of the River
Plate to put wool, hides, meat, and tallow into
the market at a lower cost for production than
any other young country, and pay with ease
rátes of interest for the loan of money, which
English people would regard as exorbitant.
The normal rate of interest charged on over-
drawn current accounts at the English banks
is nine per cent., though by special arrangement advances may be obtained at the lower
rate of eight per cent.   The common rate at

which the people of the country lend to each other is twelve per cent., and in many cases as much as eighteen per cent. is paid for loans which in England would be readily advanced at five per cent. It is quite obvious from the punctuality with which the interest is paid, that these high rates are not really unfair to the borrower, however extortionate they may appear to us.

Many persons look with distrust on South American investments, merely on account of their carrying high rates of interest. How can a country, or a province, or a company, pay its way that offers 100*l.* bonds carrying six per cent. interest at 85*l.* or 90*l.* each ? is a question English investors often ask with natural suspicion. I must admit that I often asked the same question myself before I visited the River Plate. Now that I have seen the country and know what rates of interest the people there readily pay to each other for advances, I can understand that loans on such terms may not only be satisfactory to the English lender, but profitable to the River Plate borrower. There

may be, and naturally are, dishonest governments and dishonest companies and dishonest
individuals in South America, just as elsewhere ; but, granted straightforward dealing
and good management, there is no reason
whatever, why the high rates of interest promised by the borrowers of the River Plate,
should not be punctually paid, quite as easily
as the lower rates we pay for similar accommodation in England. Good investments in
the Plate cannot of course be selected at
random, any more than they can elsewhere, but
if chosen with judgment and knowledge, they
will yield the investor steady dividends, and
an increasing capital value.

Many persons of discretion, who invest
largely in solid commercial undertakings, are
shy of the Government securities, and distrust
the finance of the politicians. There is this
much to be said in favour of the national
securities, that the United States is the ideal
of the rulers of the Argentine Confederation.
They look to that country as presenting the
true picture of human happiness, and soldiers

and wars which drain away the earnings of the workers to support in idleness those who should be adding to the common stock of human requirements, are not regarded by them in any degree as subjects for satisfaction, much less for glorification as the stock centre-pieces of state pageants.

The ease with which a high rate of interest may be borne in a new country may perhaps be best illustrated by an example.   '

River Plate Small Farm.

	£
Farm of 1,000 acres, with necessary buildings and fencing, costs say 1,500*l.*, which the occupant borrows at 12 per cent.	180
Export duties on produce, hides, tallow, &c. . .	30
Land Tax	8
	£218

English Farm.

Farm of 500 acres, rent	440
Tithe	60
Poor Rate	25
District Rate	10
Land Tax and Property Tax	5
	£540 .

In the above examples it will be noticed that the rent for the English farm is by no

Q

means high, being only eighteen shillings an acre. On the other hand, the River Plate farm may be taken to be good land and is double the size. Yet the River Plate farmer, borrowing at twelve per cent., is not called upon to pay nearly as much as even half what the English farmer has to pay before earning any profit for himself. It is better for the River Plate farmer to purchase his land, whatever rate of interest he may have to pay, for he can then fearlessly improve his property, every dollar he lays out being absolutely secured to him.

Although the direct taxes upon the land are light as compared with those borne by land in England, in the form of tithes, poor, highway, police, education, and other rates, very considerable taxes are levied indirectly, in the form of taxes upon the stock that the land carries. The municipalities levy on every head of cattle that is killed for consumption ·a tax of one dollar (four shillings), and on every sheep twenty cents (tenpence). These taxes are decidedly heavy, if we bear in mind what a large proportion they bear to the value of the animals in the River Plate. A cow or sheep is worth, in England, as many pounds as in the River Plate it would be worth dollars ; so that, for purposes of comparison, a duty of a dollar in the River Plate is equivalent to a duty of one pound in England. There is, moreover, a tax of 6 per cent. upon all wool, sheepskins, hides, tallow, bones, horns, and meat exported. These taxes add something considerable to the cost of production, though, no doubt, they do not equal in amount that which the English farmer is called upon in the aggregate to pay.

One thing that struck me with some surprise in connection with the high rate of interest paid in South America, is the low rate of interest earned for their shareholders, by the English banks banking in South America. With such a field for their operations, I can hardly understand how it is they do not pay higher dividends. The four English banks, in Brazil and the River Plate, yield their shareholders on the average about 10

per cent. Yet in England many English
banks pay 20 per cent., and after full allow-
ance for everything in the way of more ex-
pensive staffs, it still appears to me that
the English banks in South America, ought to
yield at least as much as the most successful
English banks, even if they do not succeed in
yielding more. With such favourable opportunities as they have, one would imagine that
they would make heavy profits ; perhaps their
profits are eaten up by losses.

The province of Buenos Ayres has established a land mortgage bank, which is getting
known in this country through its mortgage
bonds known as Cedulas (Cĕdŭlas). The
bank advances money upon the security of
land to one half its assessed value, and the
Cedulas are the bonds issued to the borrowers
at par in lieu of cash.

This method of borrowing is not very
satisfactory, for two reasons. An estanciero
borrows, say, $20,000 on his landed property,
and is handed Cedulas for $20,000 by the
bank, bearing 8 per cent. interest. Cedulas

are selling at a discount, and for his $20,000 he may only realise $18,000. When the time of repayment comes, he has the option of making repayment in cash at par, or of purchasing in the market Cedulas of the same issue, of an equivalent amount to those issued to him. But in the meantime the value of Cedulas may have risen, so that when the time for repayment comes, the borrower can never be certain that he may not be called upon to pay considerably more than he has received. There is, moreover (in addition to the interest on the Cedulas), a commission of 1 per cent., payable to the bank, on the whole loan, as long as any part of it is outstanding. This is a severe tax. For example, A borrows $20,000 at 8 per cent. ; the interest he has to pay is $1,600 a year, plus $200 a year for commission, or 9 per cent. He pays off gradually $15,000 of the advance, and remains liable for $400 a year interest on the unpaid $5,000, plus $200 a year commission on the whole loan. He is then paying at the rate of 12 per cent. for the unpaid portion of his advance. To raise money to make these advances to mortgagors, the bank has created a series of bonds to the amount of some thirteen millions sterling, bearing interest at rates varying from 6 to 8 per cent. The National Bank of the Republic has issued bonds of a similar kind. The Cedulas of the Provincial Bank at Buenos Ayres, are guaranteed by the Provincial Government, and the Cedulas of the National Bank by the Federal Government. One cannot help feeling that mortgages may be repaid and that the equivalent Cedulas may not be called in and cancelled, and that more Cedulas may thus remain in the hands of investors than the mortgages warrant. Some grave scandals of this kind came to light not long ago. Such securities may be suitable for those who dwell in the country, but hardly seem to be the best class of investment for foreign investors, as the banks do not in any way ear-mark the securities on which the purchasers of Cedulas rely for the eventual realisation of their bonds.

The countries of the River Plate .have

prospered greatly, and with good government will doubtless continue to prosper, for many years to come ; yet there are troubles likely to arise in the future, and it is not difficult to see where the shoe will pinch. Unless the statesmen of these countries are wise in time, troubles will ensue from the landowners being permitted to hold land in unlimited quantity. The rural population is scanty for the size of the country, and owing to the large holdings, does not increase in proportion to the power of the country to maintain an increased population.

The land in many parts is parcelled out into huge estates, varying in size from ten to thirty square miles in extent, occupied by innumerable herds and flocks, but tenanted as far as humanity goes, only by a few herdsmen and shepherds, to look after the stock. These great estancias are peopled by perhaps five-and-twenty persons all told, while much of the land would easily carry from twelve to fifteen families to the square mile. Several colonies have been started with forty acres to a family, and

upon this amount of land the settlers are
doing well. There are thousands of leagues of
country now carrying one or two, or at most
three persons to the square mile, which would
easily maintain in comfort seventy to eighty
persons to the square mile. Thousands of
miles are crying out for people to go and dig
them, but they do not and cannot go, until
the State rouses itself to the effort of facilitat-
ing the acquirement of small holdings by the
peasant class. Many of the capitalist landowners are absentees—off-abiders, as Barnes,
the Dorset poor-man's poet, used to term them
in his vigorous Saxon—and many more are
preparing to follow their evil example. The
great landowners are so abundantly well to do,
that they can afford to be idle, and as means
of amusement are more abundant in older
countries, they naturally betake themselves
thither. The poor labourers remain while the
rich depart to drain away the wealth of the
country : nothing can be more disastrous.
Happily as yet one can only discern the
beginnings of this evil state of things. But

the rulers of these lands will have to mark these things well, and find a remedy. They may do this by a stern application of the law of expropriation, by which large holders may be bought out by the State at the market rate, and their lands colonised by small owners.

In the United States the homestead law, which strictly limits the amount which new comers may take up, has prevented great capitalists from appropriating enormous areas of land which they are able merely to hold, and quite unable to develop. In the River Plate countries, provided certain conditions of a comparatively easy kind are complied with, relating to fencing in the land, there is practically no limit to the gorge of the capitalist landowner. When once a big land-owner is in possession, the powers that be, shrink from applying the laws of expropria-tion. Mammoth landowners are allowed to take up vast tracts of land on the supposition, that when the land is required for a more numerous body of smaller owners, the State will expropriate the larger owners in favour of smaller ones. But the large owners are powerful, and the statesmen of these countries flinch from making a move against them. The situation is no doubt a difficult one, yet one cannot help feeling that, having made the error of allowing landowners to straightway possess themselves of gigantic estates, the State will sooner or later have to face courageously the difficulty of applying a remedy to this state of things.

The true strength and stability of a country lies in an industrious well-to-do resident population. But to assist the growth of small landowners good means of communication are essential. Small proprietors cannot horse and coach themselves over scores of miles of muddy rut-ploughed tracks in a land where no regular conveyances run. For the purposes of improving communication, Governments must borrow of the foreign capitalist; and provided these loans are steadily repaid by means of sinking funds, so that the country does not continue permanently indebted to the foreign lender, such loans will benefit the borrowing

community. There is no virtue in foreign
capital unless it is in the first place well
applied, and in the second place repaid within
reasonable limits of time. Loans to new
countries on such terms bless both those that
lend and those that borrow.

It seems strange that such young countries
should so soon be threatened with a land question, but the indifference of Governments to a
reasonable limitation of the size of properties,
and the dog-in-the-
manger greed of big
capitalists who grasp
at large areas of land,
in order that they may
demand   exorbitant
prices for their unim-
proved holdings, is
not a practice pecu-
liar to the River Plate.

BIRD ROCK LIGHT, CAPE
DE VERD.

But I have said
enough of these things, and the puffing,
bustling little steam launch is waiting, to
hurry us from the Boca over three leagues

of water to the homeward-bound 'Trent.' Once again we travelled along the 2,000 miles of coast to Pernambuco, calling at many ports. After leaving Pernambuco we broke our mid-Atlantic journey to coal at the Cape de Verd (green) Islands, a beautiful necklet of isles.

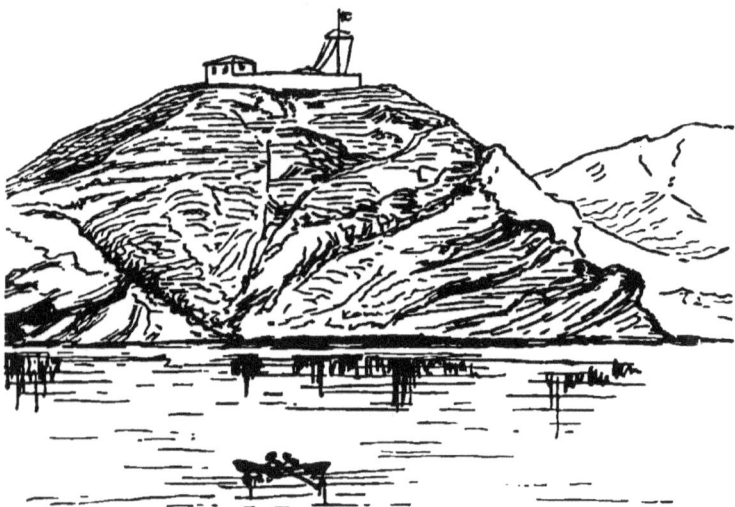

LOOK-OUT STATION, ST. VINCENT.

Their arid shores and spiky crests could hardly look more enchanting than on the evening we anchored off St. Vincent, blue-black against a glowing crimson sky. In the morning we were awakened by the screech of the donkey engine, to find our cabin insufferably hot, owing to the portholes being tightly barred against the insidious inroad of clouds of coal dust. But this passing inconvenience was soon over, the time being wiled away in chaffering over the ship's side, for trifles which the Islanders had doubtless imported from Birmingham.

Then the whistle sounded, the anchor weighed, and once again we were

> Upon the thousand waves of sea
> That ripple round the lonely ship.

INDEX.

R

PRINTED BY
SPOTTISWOODE AND CO., NEW-STREET SQUARE
LONDON

A LIST OF BOOKS

PUBLISHED BY

CHATTO & WINDUS,

214, PICCADILLY, LONDON, W.

Sold by all Booksellers, or sent post-free for the published price by the Publishers.

About.—The Fellah: An Egyptian Novel. By EDMOND ABOUT. Translated by Sir RANDAL ROBERTS. Post 8vo, illustrated boards, 2s. ; cloth limp, 2s. 6d.

Adams (W. Davenport), Works by:

A Dictionary of the Drama. Being a comprehensive Guide to the Plays, Playwrights, Players, and Playhouses of the United Kingdom and America, from the Earliest to the Present Times. Crown 8vo, half-bound, 12s. 6d. [*Preparing.*

Quips and Quiddities. Selected by W. DAVENPORT ADAMS. Post 8vo, cloth limp, 2s. 6d.

Advertising, A History of, from the Earliest Times. Illustrated by Anecdotes, Curious Specimens, and Notices of Successful Advertisers. By HENRY SAMPSON. Crown 8vo, with Coloured Frontispiece and Illustrations, cloth gilt, 7s. 6d.

Agony Column (The) of "The Times," from 1800 to 1870. Edited, with an Introduction, by ALICE CLAY. Post 8vo, cloth limp, 2s. 6d.

Aïdé (Hamilton), Works by: Post 8vo, illustrated boards, 2s each.

Carr of Carrlyon. | Confidences.

Alexander (Mrs.), Novels by: Post 8vo, illustrated boards, 2s. each.

Maid, Wife, or Widow ?
Valerie's Fate.

Allen (Grant), Works by: Crown 8vo, cloth extra, 6s. each.

The Evolutionist at Large. Second Edition, revised.
Vignettes from Nature.
Colin Clout's Calendar.

ALLEN (GRANT)—*continued.*

Strange Stories. With Frontispiece by GEORGE DU MAURIER. Cr. 8vo, cl. ex., 6s. ; post 8vo, illust. bds., 2s.

Philistia: A Novel. Crown 8vo, cloth limp, 2s. 6d. ; post 8vo, illust. bds., 2s. extra. 3s 6d ; post 8vo, illust. bds., 2s.

Babylon· A Novel. With 12 Illusts. by P. MACNAB. Crown 8vo, cloth extra, 3s. 6d. ; post 8vo, illust. bds , 2s.

For Mamie's Sake: A Tale of Love and Dynamite. Cr. 8vo, cl. ex., 6s.

In all Shades: A Novel. New and Cheaper Edition. Crown 8vo, cloth extra, 3s. 6d.

The Beckoning Hand, &c. With a Frontispiece by TOWNLEY GREEN. Crown 8vo, cloth extra, 6s.

An Anthology of the Novels of the Century: Choice Readings from all the best Novels of the last Eighty Years. Edited, with Critical and Biographical Notes, by H. T. MACKENZIE BELL. Crown 8vo, 3s. 6d. [*Preparing.*

Architectural Styles, A Handbook of. Translated from the German of A. ROSENGARTEN, by W. COLLETT-SANDARS. Crown 8vo, cloth extra, with 639 Illustrations, 7s. 6d.

Artemus Ward:

Artemus Ward's Works: The Works of CHARLES FARRER BROWNE, better known as ARTEMUS WARD. With Portrait and Facsimile. Crown 8vo, cloth extra, 7s. 6d.

Artemus Ward's Lecture on the Mormons. With 32 Illustrations. Edited, with Preface, by EDWARD P. HINGSTON. Crown 8vo, 6d.

The Genial Showman: Life and Adventures of Artemus Ward. By EDWARD P. HINGSTON. With a Frontispiece. Cr. 8vo, cl. extra, 3s. 6d.

Arnold.—Bird Life in England.
By EDWIN LESTER ARNOLD. Crown
8vo, cloth extra. 6s.

Art (The) of Amusing: A Collection of Graceful Arts, Games, Tricks, Puzzles, and Charades. By FRANK BELLEW. With 300 Illustrations. Cr. 8vo cloth extra, 4s. 6d.

Ashton (John), Works by:
Crown 8vo, cloth extra, 7s. 6d. each.

A History of the Chap-Books of the Eighteenth Century. With nearly 400 Illustrations, engraved in facsimile of the originals.

Social Life in the Reign of Queen Anne. From Original Sources. With nearly 100 Illustrations.

Humour, Wit, and Satire of the Seventeenth Century. With nearly 100 Illustrations.

English Caricature and Satire on Napoleon the First. With 120 Illustrations from Originals. Two Vols., demy 8vo, cloth extra, 28s.

Bacteria.—A Synopsis of the
Bacteria and Yeast Fungi and Allied Species. By W. B. GROVE, B.A. With 87 Illusts. Crown 8vo, cl. extra, 3s. 6d.

Bankers, A Handbook of London; together with Lists of Bankers from 1677. By F. G. HILTON PRICE. Crown 8vo, cloth extra, 7s. 6d.

Bardsley (Rev. C.W.), Works by:
Crown 8vo, cloth extra, 7s. 6d. each.

Engl sh Surnames: Their Sources and Significations. Third Ed., revised.

Curiosities of Puritan Nomenclature.

Bartholomew Fair, Memoirs
of. By HENRY MORLEY. With 100 Illusts. Crown 8vo, cloth extra, 7s. 6d.

Beaconsfield, Lord: A Biography. By T. P. O'CONNOR. M.P. Sixth Edition with a New Preface. Crown 8vo, cloth extra, 7s. 6d.

Beauchamp. — Grantley
Grange: A Novel. By SHELSLEY BEAUCHAMP. Post 8vo, illust. bds., 2s.

Beautiful Pictures by British
Artists: A Gathering of Favourites from our Picture Galleries. All engraved on Steel in the highest style of Art. Edited, with Notices of the Artists, by SYDNEY ARMYTAGE, M.A. Imperial 4to, cloth extra, gilt and gilt edges, 21s.

Bechstein. — As Pretty as
Seven, and other German Stories. Collected by LUDWIG BECHSTEIN. With Additional Tales by the Brothers GRIMM, and 100 Illusts. by RICHTER. Small 4to, green and gold, 6s. 6d. gilt edges. 7s. 6d.

Beerbohm. — Wanderings in
Patagonia; or, Life among the Ostrich Hunters. By JULIUS BEERBOHM. With Illusts. Crown 8vo, cloth extra, 3s. 6d.

Belgravia. One Shilling Monthly. The Number for JANUARY contained Stories by WILKIE COLLINS, Miss BRADDON, Mrs. ALFRED HUNT, the Author of "Phyllis," and other Popular Authors.—A New Serial Story by W. CLARK RUSSELL, entitled The Frozen Pirate, begins in the JULY Number.

₊ Now ready, the Volume for MARCH to JUNE, 1887, cloth extra, gilt edges, 7s. 6d.; Cases for binding Vols., 2s. each.

Belgravia Holiday Number,
1887. Demy 8vo, with Illustrations, 1s.

Bennett (W.C.,LL.D.),Works by:
Post 8vo, cloth limp, 2s. each.
A Ballad History of England.
Songs for Sailors.

Besant (Walter) and James
Rice, Novels by. Crown 8vo, cloth extra, 3s. 6d. each ; post 8vo, illust. boards, 2s. each; cloth limp, 2s. 6d. each.

Ready-Money Mortiboy.
With Harp and Crown.
This Son of Vulcan.
My Little Girl.
The Case of Mr. Lucraft.
The Golden Butterfly.
By Celia's Arbour.
The Monks of Thelema.
'Twas in Trafalgar's Bay.
The Seamy Side.
The Ten Years' Tenant.
The Chaplain of the Fleet.

Besant (Walter), Novels by:
Crown 8vo, cloth extra, 3s. 6d. each ; post 8vo, illust. boards, 2s. each; cloth limp, 2s. 6d. each

All Sorts and Conditions of Men: An Impossible Story With Illustrations by FRED. BARNARD.
The Capta'ns' Room. &c. With Frontispiece by E. J. WHEELER.
All in a Garden Fair. With 6 Illusts. by H. FURNISS.
Dorothy Forster. With Frontispiece by CHARLES GREEN.
Uncle Jack, and other Stories.

BESANT, WALTER, continued—
Children of Gibeon: A Novel. New
and Cheaper Edition. Crown 8vo,
cloth extra, 3s. 6d.

The World Went Very Well Then.
With Etching of Portrait by JOHN
PETTIE, R.A., and 11 ustrations by
A. FORESTIER. Three Vols., cr. 8vo.

The Art of Fiction. Demy 8vo, 1s.

**Library Edition of the Novels of
Walter Besant & James Rice.**
Messrs. CHATTO & WINDUS have in
the press a choicely-printed Library
Edition of the Novels of Messrs. BESANT
and RICE. The Volumes (each one containing a Complete Novel) will be printed
from a specially-cast fount of type by
Messrs. BALLANTYNE & HANSON, of
the Ballantyne Press. on a large crown
8vo page, and will be issued in Six-
Shilling Monthly Volumes. handsomely
bound in cloth by Messrs. BURN & Co.
The First Volume of 512 pages (now
ready) is
Ready-Money Mortiboy,
with Portrait of JAMES RICE, etched by
DANIEL A. WEHR SCHMIDT, and a New
Preface by WALTER BESANT, telling the
story of his literary partnership with
JAMES RICE. This Novel will be followed
at regular intervals by the following:—
My Little Girl.
With Harp and Crown.
This Son of Vulcan.
The Golden Butterfly. With Etched
Portrait of WALTER BESANT.
The Monks of Thelema.
By Celia's Arbour.
The Chaplain of the Fleet.
The Seamy Side. &c. &c.

Betham-Edwards (M.), Novels
by. Crown 8vo, cloth extra, 3s. 6d.
each. ; post 8vo, illust. bds., 2s. each.
Felicia. | Kitty.

Bewick (Thos.) and his Pupils.
By AUSTIN DOBSON. With 95 Illustrations. Square 8vo, cloth extra, 10s. 6d.

Birthday Books:—
The Starry Heavens: A Poetical
Birthday Book. Square 8vo, hand-
somely bound in cloth, 2s. 6d.
Birthday Flowers: Their Language
and Legends. By W. J. GORDON.
Beautifully Illustrated in Colours by
VIOLA BOUGHTON. In illuminated
cover, crown 4to, 6s.
The Lowell Birthday Book. With
Illusts. Small 8vo, cloth extra, 4s. 6d.

Blackburn's (Henry) Art Hand-
books. Demy 8vo, Illustrated, uniform in size for binding.
Academy Notes, separate years, from
1875 to 1886, each 1s.

BLACKBURN, HENRY, continued—
Academy Notes. 1887. With nu-
merous Illustrations. 1s.
Academy Notes, 1875-79. Complete
in One Vol.,with nearly 6 00 Illusts. in
Facsimile. Demy 8vo, cloth limp, 6s.
Academy Notes, 1880-84. Complete
in One Volume, with about 700 Fac-
simile Illustrations. Cloth limp, 6s.
Grosvenor Notes, 1877. 6d.
Grosvenor Notes, separate years, from
1878 to 1886, each 1s.
Grosvenor Notes. 1887. With nu-
merous Illusts 1s.
Grosvenor Notes, 1877-82. With
upwards of 300 Illustrations. Demy
8vo, cloth limp, 6s.
Grosvenor Notes, 1883-87. With
upwards of 300 Illustrations. Demy
8vo, cloth limp, 6s. [Preparing.
Pictures at South Kensington. With
70 Illusts. 1s. [New Edit. preparing.
The English Pictures at the National
Gallery. 114 Illustrations. 1s.
The Old Masters at the National
Gallery. 125 Illustrations. 1s. 6d.
A Complete Illustrated Catalogue
to the National Gallery. With
Notes by H. BLACKBURN, and 242
Illusts. Demy 8vo, cloth limp, 3s.
Illustrated Catalogue of the Luxem-
bourg Gallery. Containing about
250 Reproductions after the Original
Drawings of the Artists. Edited by
F. G. DUMAS. Demy 8vo. 3s. 6d.
The Paris Salon, 1887. With about
300 Facsimile Sketches. Demy 8vo,3s.

Blake (William): Etchings from
his Works. By W. B. SCOTT. With
descriptive Text. Folio, half-bound
boards, India Proofs, 21s.

Boccaccio's Decameron; or,
Ten Days' Entertainment. Translated
into English. with an Introduction by
THOMAS WRIGHT, F.S.A. With Portrait
and STOTHARD'S beautiful Copper-
plates. Cr. 8vo, cloth extra, gilt, 7s. 6d.

Bowers'(G.) Hunting Sketches:
Oblong 4to, half-bound boards, 21s. each.
Canters In Crampshire.
Leaves from a Hunting Journal.
Coloured in facsimile of the originals.

Boyle (Frederick), Works by:
Crown 8vo, cloth extra, 3s. 6d. each; post
8vo, illustrated boards, 2s. each.
Camp Notes: Stories of Sport and
Adventure in Asia, Africa, and
America. [Trotter.
Savage Life: Adventures of a Globe-
Chronicles of No-Man's Land
Post 8vo, illust. boards, 2s.

Brand's Observations on Popular Antiquities, chiefly Illustrating the Origin of our Vulgar Customs, Ceremonies, and Superstitions. With the Additions of Sir HENRY ELLIS. Crown 8vo, cloth extra, gilt, with numerous Illustrations, 7s. 6d.

Bret Harte, Works by:
Bret Harte's Collected Works. Arranged and Revised by the Author. Complete in Five Vols., crown 8vo, cloth extra, 6s. each.
Vol. I. COMPLETE POETICAL AND DRAMATIC WORKS. With Steel Portrait, and Introduction by Author.
Vol. II. EARLIER PAPERS—LUCK OF ROARING CAMP, and other Sketches —BOHEMIAN PAPERS — SPANISH AND AMERICAN LEGENDS.
Vol. III. TALES OF THE ARGONAUTS —EASTERN SKETCHES.
Vol. IV. GABRIEL CONROY.
Vol. V. STORIES — CONDENSED NOVELS, &c.
The Select Works of Bret Harte, in Prose and Poetry. With Introductory Essay by J. M. BELLEW. Portrait of the Author, and 50 Illustrations. Crown 8vo cloth extra. 7s. 6d.
Bret Harte's Complete Poetical Works. Author's Copyright Edition. Beautifully printed on hand-made paper and bound in buckram. Cr. 8vo, 4s. 6d.
Gabriel Conroy: A Novel. Post 8vo, illustrated boards, 2s.
An Heiress of Red Dog, and other Stories. Post 8vo, illust. boards. 2s.
The Twins of Table Mountain. Fcap. 8vo, picture cover, 1s.
Luck of Roaring Camp, and other Sketches. Post 8vo, illust. bds., 2s.
Jeff Briggs's Love Story. Fcap 8vo, picture cover. 1s. [2s. 6d.
Flip. Post 8vo, illust. bds., 2s.; cl. limp,
Californian Stories (including THE TWINS OF TABLE MOUNTAIN, JEFF BRIGGS'S LOVE STORY, &c.) Post 8vo, illustrated boards, 2s.
Maruja: A Novel. Post 8vo, illust. boards, 2s.; cloth limp, 2s. 6d.
The Queen of the Pirate Isle. With 28 original Drawings by KATE GREENAWAY, Reproduced in Colours by EDMUND EVANS. Sm. 4to, bds., 5s.

Brewer (Rev. Dr.), Works by:
The Reader's Handbook of Allusions, References, Plots, and Stories. Fifth Edition, revised throughout, with a New Appendix, containing a COMPLETE ENGLISH BIBLIOGRAPHY. Cr. 8vo, 1,400 pp., cloth extra, 7s. 6d.
Authors and their Works, with the Dates: Being the Appendices to "The Reader's Handbook," separately printed. Cr. 8vo, cloth limp, 2s.

BREWER (REV. DR.), *continued—*
A Dictionary of Miracles: Imitative, Realistic, and Dogmatic. Crown 8vo, cloth extra, 7s. 6d.; half-bound, 9s.

Brewster(Sir David),Works by:
More Worlds than One: The Creed of the Philosopher and the Hope of the Christian. With Plates. Post 8vo, cloth extra, 4s. 6d.
The Martyrs of Science: Lives of GALILEO, TYCHO BRAHE, and KEPLER. With Portraits. Post 8vo, cloth extra, 4s. 6d.
Letters on Natural Magic. A New Edition, with numerous Illustrations, and Chapters on the Being and Faculties of Man, and Additional Phenomena of Natural Magic, by J. A. SMITH. Post 8vo, cl. ex., 4s. 6d.

Briggs, Memoir of Gen. John.
By Major EVANS BELL. With a Portrait. Royal 8vo, cloth extra, 7s. 6d.

Brillat-Savarin.—Gastronomy
as a Fine Art. By BRILLAT-SAVARIN. Translated by R. E. ANDERSON, M.A. Post 8vo, cloth limp, 2s. 6d.

Buchanan's (Robert) Works:
Crown 8vo, cloth extra, 6s. each.
Ballads of Life, Love, and Humour. Frontispiece by ARTHUR HUGHES.
Undertones. | London Poems.
The Book of Orm.
White Rose and Red: A Love Story.
Idylls and Legends of Inverburn.
Selected Poems of Robert Buchanan With a Frontispiece by T. DALZIEL.
The Hebrid Isles: Wanderings in the Land of Lorne and the Outer Hebrides. With Frontispiece by WILLIAM SMALL.
A Poet's Sketch-Book: Selections from the Prose Writings of ROBERT BUCHANAN.
The Earthquake; or, Six Days and a Sabbath. Cr. 8vo, cloth extra, 6s.
Robert Buchanan's Complete Poetical Works. With Steel-plate Portrait. Crown 8vo, cloth extra, 7s. 6d.

Crown 8vo, cloth extra, 3s. 6d. each; post 8vo, illust. boards, 2s. each.
The Shadow of the Sword.
A Child of Nature. With a Frontispiece.
God and the Man. With Illustrations by FRED. BARNARD.
The Martyrdom of Madeline. With Frontispiece by A. W. COOPER.
Love Me for Ever. With a Frontispiece by P. MACNAB.
Annan Water. | The New Abelard.
Foxglove Manor.
Matt: A Story of a Caravan.
The Master of the Mine.

Bunyan's Pilgrim's Progress.
Edited by Rev. T. SCOTT. With 17 Steel Plates by STOTHARD engraved by GOODALL, and numerous Woodcuts. Crown 8vo, cloth extra, gilt, 7s. 6d.

Burnett (Mrs.), Novels by:
Surly Tim, and other Stories. Post 8vo, illustrated boards, 2s.

Fcap. 8vo, picture cover, 1s. each.
Kathleen Mavourneen.
Lindsay's Luck.
Pretty Polly Pemberton.

Burton (Captain), Works by:
To the Gold Coast for Gold: A Personal Narrative. By RICHARD F. BURTON and VERNEY LOVETT CAMERON. With Maps and Frontispiece. Two Vols., crown 8vo, cloth extra, 21s.

The Book of the Sword: Being a History of the Sword and its Use in all Countries, from the Earliest Times. By RICHARD F. BURTON. With over 400 Illustrations. Square 8vo, cloth extra, 32s.

Burton (Robert):
The Anatomy of Melancholy. A New Edition, complete, corrected and enriched by Translations of the Classical Extracts. Demy 8vo, cloth extra, 7s. 6d.

Melancholy Anatomised: Being an Abridgment, for popular use, of BURTON'S ANATOMY OF MELANCHOLY. Post 8vo, cloth limp, 2s. 6d.

Byron (Lord):
Byron's Childe Harold. An entirely New Edition of this famous Poem, with over One Hundred new Illusts. by leading Artists. (Uniform with the Illustrated Editions of "The Lady of the Lake" and "Marmion.") Elegantly and appropriately bound, small 4to, 16s.

Byron's Letters and Journals. With Notices of his Life. By THOMAS MOORE. A Reprint of the Original Edition. Cr. 8vo, cloth extra, 7s. 6d.

Byron's Don Juan. Complete in One Vol., post 8vo, cloth limp, 2s.

Caine (T. Hall), Novels by:
The Shadow of a Crime. Cr. 8vo, cloth extra, 3s. 6d.; post 8vo, illustrated boards, 2s.

A Son of Hagar. New and Cheaper Edition. Crown 8vo, cloth extra, 3s. 6d.

Cameron (Comdr.), Works by:
To the Gold Coast for Gold: A Personal Narrative. By RICHARD F. BURTON and VERNEY LOVETT CAMERON. With Frontispiece and Maps. Two Vols., crown 8vo, cloth extra, 21s.

The Cruise of the "Black Prince" Privateer, Commanded by ROBERT HAWKINS, Master Mariner. By Commander V. LOVETT CAMERON R.N., C.B., D.C.L. With Frontis piece and Vignette by P. MACNAB Crown 8vo, cl. ex., 5s.

Cameron (Mrs. H. Lovett),
Novels by:
Crown 8vo, cloth extra, 3s. 6d. each post 8vo, illustrated boards, 2s. each.
Juliet's Guardian. | Deceivers Ever.

Carlyle (Thomas):
On the Choice of Books. By THOMAS CARLYLE. With a Life of the Author by R. H. SHEPHERD. New and Revised Edition, post 8vo, cloth extra, Illustrated, 1s. 6d.

The Correspondence of Thomas Carlyle and Ralph Waldo Emerson, 1834 to 1872. Edited by CHARLES ELIOT NORTON. With Portraits. Two Vols., crown 8vo, cloth extra, 24s.

Chapman's (George) Works:
Vol. I. contains the Plays complete, including the doubtful ones. Vol. II., the Poems and Minor Translations, with an Introductory Essay by ALGERNON CHARLES SWINBURNE. Vol. III., the Translations of the Iliad and Odyssey. Three Vols., crown 8vo, cloth extra, 18s.; or separately, 6s. each.

Chatto & Jackson.—A Treatise
on Wood Engraving, Historical and Practical. By WM. ANDREW CHATTO and JOHN JACKSON. With an Additional Chapter by HENRY G. BOHN; and 450 fine Illustrations. A Reprint of the last Revised Edition. Large 4to, half-bound, 28s.

Chaucer:
Chaucer for Children: A Golden Key. By Mrs. H R. HAWEIS. Eight Coloured Pictures and numerous Woodcuts by the Author. New Ed., small 4to, cloth extra, 6s.
Chaucer for Schools. By Mrs. H. R. HAWEIS. Demy 8vo, cloth limp, 2s. 6d.

Chronicle (The) of the Coach:
Charing Cross to Ilfracombe. By J. D CHAMPLIN. With 75 Illustrations by EDWARD L. CHICHESTER. Square 8vo, cloth extra, 7s. 6d.

City (The) of Dream: A Poem.
Fcap. 8vo, cloth extra, 6s. [In the press.

Clodd. — Myths and Dreams.
By EDWARD CLODD, F.R.A.S., Author
of "The Childhood of Religions," &c.
Crown 8vo, cloth extra, 5s.

Cobban.—The Cure of Souls:
A Story. By J. MACLAREN COBBAN.
Post 8vo, illustrated boards, 2s.

Coleman.—Curly: An Actor's
Story. By JOHN COLEMAN. Illustrated
by J. C. DOLLMAN. Crown 8vo, 1s.;
cloth, 1s. 6d.

Collins (Wilkie), Novels by:
Crown 8vo, cloth extra, Illustrated,
3s. 6d. each; post 8vo, illustrated bds.,
2s. each; cloth limp, 2s. 6d. each.
Antonina. Illust. by Sir JOHN GILBERT.
Basil. Illustrated by Sir JOHN GIL-
BERT and J. MAHONEY.
Hide and Seek. Illustrated by Sir
JOHN GILBERT and J. MAHONEY.
The Dead Secret. Illustrated by Sir
JOHN GILBERT.
Queen of Hearts. Illustrated by Sir
JOHN GILBERT.
My Miscellanies. With a Steel-plate
Portrait of WILKIE COLLINS.
The Woman In White. With Illus-
trations by Sir JOHN GILBERT and
F. A. FRASER.
The Moonstone. With Illustrations
by G. DU MAURIER and F. A. FRASER.
Man and Wife. Illust. by W. SMALL.
Poor Miss Finch. Illustrated by
G. DU MAURIER and EDWARD
HUGHES.
Miss or Mrs.? With Illustrations by
S. L. FILDES and HENRY WOODS.
The New Magdalen. Illustrated by
G. DU MAURIER and C. S. REINHARDT.
The Frozen Deep. Illustrated by
G. DU MAURIER and J. MAHONEY.
The Law and the Lady. Illustrated
by S. L. FILDES and SYDNEY HALL.
The Two Destinies.
The Haunted Hotel. Illustrated by
ARTHUR HOPKINS.
The Fallen Leaves.
Jezebel's Daughter.
The Black Robe.
Heart and Science: A Story of the
Present Time.
"I Say No."
The Evil Genius.

Little Novels. Three Vols., cr. 8vo.

Collins (Mortimer), Novels by:
Crown 8vo, cloth extra, 3s. 6d. each; post
8vo, illustrated boards, 2s. each.

Sweet Anne Page. | Transmigration.
From Midnight to Midnight.

A Fight with Fortune. Post 8vo,
illustrated boards, 2s.

Collins (Mortimer & Frances),
Novels by:
Crown 8vo, cloth extra, 3s. 6d. each; post
8vo, illustrated boards, 2s. each.
Blacksmith and Scholar.
The Village Comedy.
You Play Me False.

Post 8vo, illustrated boards, 2s. each.
Sweet and Twenty. | Frances.

Collins (C. Allston).—The Bar
Sinister: A Story. By C. ALLSTON
COLLINS. Post 8vo, illustrated bds., 2s.

Colman's Humorous Works:
"Broad Grins," "My Nightgown and
Slippers," and other Humorous Works,
Prose and Poetical, of GEORGE COL-
MAN. With Life by G. B. BUCKSTONE,
and Frontispiece by HOGARTH. Crown
8vo cloth extra, gilt, 7s. 6d.

Convalescent Cookery: A
Family Handbook. By CATHERINE
RYAN. Crown 8vo, 1s.; cloth, 1s. 6d.

Conway (Moncure D.), Works
by:
Demonology and Devil-Lore. Two
Vols., royal 8vo, with 65 Illusts., 28s.
A Necklace of Stories. Illustrated
by W. J. HENNESSY. Square 8vo,
cloth extra, 6s.

Cook (Dutton), Works by:
Crown 8vo, cloth extra, 6s each.
Hours with the Players. With a
Steel Plate Frontispiece.
Nights at the Play: A View of the
English Stage.

Leo: A Novel. Post 8vo, illustrated
boards, 2s.
Paul Foster's Daughter. crown 8vo,
cloth extra, 3s. 6d.; post 8vo, illustrated boards, 2s.

Copyright. — A Handbook of
English and Foreign Copyright In
Literary and Dramatic Works. By
SIDNEY JERROLD, of the Middle
Temple, Esq., Barrister-at-Law. Post
8vo, cloth limp, 2s. 6d.

Cornwall.—PopularRomances
of the West of England; or, The
Drolls, Traditions, and Superstitions
of Old Cornwall. Collected and Edited
by ROBERT HUNT, F.R.S. New and
Revised Edition, with Additions, and
Two Steel-plate Illustrations by
GEORGE CRUIKSHANK. Crown 8vo,
cloth extra, 7s. 6d.

Craddock. — The Prophet of
the Great Smoky Mountains. By
CHARLES EGBERT CRADDOCK. Post
8vo, illust. bds., 2s.; cloth limp, 2s. 6d.

Creasy.—Memoirs of Eminent Etonians : with Notices of the Early History of Eton College. By Sir EDWARD CREASY, Author of " The Fifteen Decisive Battles of the World." Crown 8vo, cloth extra, gilt, with 13 Portraits, 7s. 6d.

Cruikshank (George):
The Comic Almanack. Complete in Two SERIES : The FIRST from 1835 to 1843; the SECOND from 1844 to 1853. A Gathering of the BEST HUMOUR of THACKERAY, HOOD, MAY-HEW, ALBERT SMITH, A'BECKETT, ROBERT BROUGH, &c. With 2,000 Woodcuts and Steel Engravings by CRUIKSHANK, HINE, LANDELLS, &c. Crown 8vo, cloth gilt, two very thick volumes, 7s. 6d. each.

The Life of George Cruikshank. By BLANCHARD JERROLD, Author of "The Life of Napoleon III.," &c. With 84 Illustrations. New and Cheaper Edition, enlarged, with Additional Plates, and a very carefully compiled Bibliography. Crown 8vo, cloth extra, 7s. 6d.

Robinson Crusoe. A beautiful reproduction of Major's Edition, with 37 Woodcuts and Two Steel Plates by GEORGE CRUIKSHANK, choicely printed. Crown 8vo, cloth extra, 7s. 6d.

Cumming (C. F. Gordon), Works by:
Demy 8vo, cloth extra, 8s. 6d. each.
In the Hebrides. With Autotype Facsimile and numerous full-page Illustrations. ————
In the Himalayas and on the Indian Plains. With numerous Illustrations. ————
Via Cornwall to Egypt. With a Photogravure Frontispiece. Demy 8vo, cloth extra, 7s. 6d.

Cussans.—Handbook of Heraldry; with Instructions for Tracing Pedigrees and Deciphering Ancient MSS., &c. By JOHN E. CUSSANS. Entirely New and Revised Edition, illustrated with over 400 Woodcuts and Coloured Plates. Crown 8vo, cloth extra, 7s. 6d.

Cyples.—Hearts of Gold: A Novel. By WILLIAM CYPLES. Crown 8vo, cloth extra, 3s. 6d. ; post 8vo, illustrated boards, 2s.

Daniel. — Merrie England in the Olden Time. By GEORGE DANIEL. With Illustrations by ROBT. CRUIKSHANK. Crown 8vo, cloth extra, 3s. 6d.

Daudet.—The Evangelist ; or, Port Salvation. By ALPHONSE DAUDET. Translated by C. HARRY MELTZER. With Portrait of the Author. Crown 8vo, cloth extra, 3s. 6d.; post 8vo, illust. boards, 2s.

Davenant. — What shall my Son be ? Hints for Parents on the Choice of a Profession or Trade for their Sons. By FRANCIS DAVENANT, M.A. Post 8vo, cloth limp, 2s. 6d.

Davies (Dr. N. E.), Works by :
Crown 8vo, 1s. each ; cloth limp, 1s. 6d. each.
One Thousand Medical Maxims.
Nursery Hints: A Mother's Guide.
Aids to Long Life. Crown 8vo, 2s. ; cloth limp, 2s. 6d.

Davies' (Sir John) Complete Poetical Works, including Psalms I. to L. in Verse, and other hitherto Unpublished MSS., for the first time Collected and Edited, with Memorial-Introduction and Notes, by the Rev. A. B. GROSART, D.D. Two Vols. crown 8vo, cloth boards, 12s.

De Maistre.—A Journey Round My Room. By XAVIER DE MAISTRE. Translated by HENRY ATTWELL. Post 8vo, cloth limp, 2s. 6d.

De Mille.—A Castle in Spain: A Novel. By JAMES DE MILLE. With a Frontispiece. Crown 8vo, cloth extra, 3s. 6d. ; post 8vo, illust. bds., 2s.

Derwent (Leith), Novels by :
Crown 8vo, cloth extra, 3s. 6d. each; post 8vo, illustrated boards, 2s. each.
Our Lady of Tears.
Circe's Lovers.

Dickens (Charles), Novels by :
Post 8vo, illustrated boards, 2s. each.

Sketches by Boz. | Nicholas Nickleby.
Pickwick Papers. | Oliver Twist.

The Speeches of Charles Dickens, 1841-1870. With a New Bibliography, revised and enlarged. Edited and Prefaced by RICHARD HERNE SHEPHERD. Crown 8vo, cloth extra, 6s.— Also a SMALLER EDITION, in the Mayfair Library. Post 8vo, cloth limp, 2s. 6d.

About England with Dickens. By ALFRED RIMMER. With 57 Illustrations by C. A. VANDERHOOF, ALFRED RIMMER, and others. Sq. 8vo, cloth extra, 10s. 6d.

Dictionaries:
A Dictionary of Miracles: Imitative, Realistic, and Dogmatic. By the Rev. E. C. BREWER, LL.D. Crown 8vo, cloth extra, 7s. 6d.; hf.-bound, 9s.

DICTIONARIES—*continued*.

The Reader's Handbook of Allusions, References, Plots, and Stories. By the Rev. E. C. BREWER, LL.D. Fifth Edition, revised throughout, with a New Appendix, containing a Complete English Bibliography. Crown 8vo, 1,400 pages, cloth extra, 7s. 6d.

Authors and their Works, with the Dates. Being the Appendices to "The Reader's Handbook," separately printed. By the Rev. Dr. BREWER. Crown 8vo, cloth limp, 2s.

Familiar Allusions: A Handbook of Miscellaneous Information; including the Names of Celebrated Statues, Paintings, Palaces, Country Seats, Ruins, Churches, Ships, Streets, Clubs, Natural Curiosities, and the like. By WM. A. WHEELER and CHARLES G. WHEELER. Demy 8vo, cloth extra, 7s. 6d.

Familiar Short Sayings of Great Men. With Historical and Explanatory Notes. By SAMUEL A. BENT, M.A. Fifth Edition, revised and enlarged. Cr. 8vo, cloth extra, 7s 6d.

A Dictionary of the Drama: Being a comprehensive Guide to the Plays, Playwrights, Players, and Playhouses of the United Kingdom and America, from the Earliest to the Present Times. By W. DAVENPORT ADAMS. A thick volume, crown 8vo, half-bound, 12s. 6d. [*In preparation*.

The Slang Dictionary: Etymological, Historical, and Anecdotal. Crown 8vo, cloth extra, 6s. 6d.

Women of the Day: A Biographical Dictionary. By FRANCES HAYS. Cr. 8vo, cloth extra, 5s.

Words, Facts, and Phrases: A Dictionary of Curious, Quaint, and Out-of-the-Way Matters. By ELIEZER EDWARDS. New and Cheaper Issue. Cr. 8vo, cl ex., 7s. 6d.; hf.-bd., 9s.

Diderot.—The Paradox of Acting. Translated, with Annotations, from Diderot's "Le Paradoxe sur le Comédien," by WALTER HERRIES POLLOCK. With a Preface by HENRY IRVING. Cr. 8vo, in parchment, 4s. 6d.

Dobson (W. T.), Works by:
Post 8vo, cloth limp, 2s. 6d. each.
Literary Frivolities, Fancies, Follies, and Frolics.
Poetical Ingenuities and Eccentricities.

Doran. — Memories of our Great Towns; with Anecdotic Gleanings concerning their Worthies and their Oddities. By Dr. JOHN DORAN, F.S.A. With 38 Illustrations. New and Cheaper Edition. Crown 8vo, cloth extra, 7s. 6d.

Drama, A Dictionary of the. Being a comprehensive Guide to the Plays, Playwrights, Players, and Playhouses of the United Kingdom and America, from the Earliest to the Present Times. By W. DAVENPORT ADAMS. (Uniform with BREWER'S "Reader's Handbook.") Crown 8vo, half-bound, 12s. 6d. [*In preparation*.

Dramatists, The Old. Cr. 8vo, cl. ex., Vignette Portraits, 6s. per Vol.
Ben Jonson's Works. With Notes Critical and Explanatory, and a Biographical Memoir by WM. GIFFORD. Edit. by Col. CUNNINGHAM. 3 Vols.
Chapman's Works. Complete in Three Vols. Vol. I. contains the Plays complete, including doubtful ones; Vol. II., Poems and Minor Translations, with Introductory Essay by A. C. SWINBURNE; Vol. III., Translations of the Iliad and Odyssey.
Marlowe's Works. Including his Translations. Edited, with Notes and Introduction, by Col. CUNNINGHAM. One Vol.
Massinger's Plays. From the Text of WILLIAM GIFFORD. Edited by Col. CUNNINGHAM. One Vol.

Dyer. — The Folk - Lore of Plants. By Rev. T. F. THISELTON DYER, M.A. Crown 8vo, cloth extra, 7s. 6d. [*In preparation*.

Early English Poets. Edited, with Introductions and Annotations, by Rev. A. B. GROSART, D.D. Crown 8vo, cloth boards, 6s. per Volume.
Fletcher's (Giles, B.D.) Complete Poems. One Vol.
Davies' (Sir John) Complete Poetical Works. Two Vols.
Herrick's (Robert) Complete Collected Poems. Three Vols.
Sidney's (Sir Philip) Complete Poetical Works. Three Vols.

Herbert (Lord) of Cherbury's Poems. Edited, with Introduction, by J. CHURTON COLLINS. Crown 8vo, parchment, 8s.

Edgcumbe. — Zephyrus: A Holiday in South America and on the River Plate. By E. R. PEARCE EDGCUMBE. With 41 Illustrations. Crown 8vo, cloth extra, 6s. [*Preparing*.

Edwardes (Mrs. A.), Novels by:
A Point of Honour. Post 8vo, illustrated boards, 2s.
Archie Lovell. Crown 8vo, cloth extra, 3s 6d.; post 8vo, illust. bds., 2s.

Eggleston.—Roxy: A Novel. By EDWARD EGGLESTON. Post 8vo, illust. boards, 2s.

Emanuel.—On Diamonds and Precious Stones: their History, Value, and Properties ; with Simple Tests for ascertaining their Reality. By HARRY EMANUEL, F.R.G.S. With numerous Illustrations, tinted and plain. Crown 8vo, cloth extra, gilt, 6s.

English Merchants: Memoirs in Illustration of the Progress of British Commerce. By H. R. FOX BOURNE. With Illusts. New and Cheaper Edit, revised. Crown 8vo, cloth extra, 7s. 6d.

Ewald (Alex. Charles, F.S.A.), Works by:
The Life and Times of Prince Charles Stuart, Count of Albany, commonly called the Young Pretender. From the State Papers and other Sources. New and Cheaper Edition, with a Portrait, crown 8vo, cloth extra, 7s. 6d.
Stories from the State Papers. With an Autotype Facsimile. Crown 8vo, cloth extra, 6s.
Studies Re-studied: Historical Sketches from Original Sources. Demy 8vo, cloth extra, 12s.

Eyes, Our : How to Preserve Them from Infancy to Old Age. By JOHN BROWNING, F.R.A.S., &c. Fifth Edition. With 55 Illustrations. Crown 8vo, cloth, 1s.

Fairholt.—Tobacco : Its History and Associations; with an Account of the Plant and its Manufacture, and its Modes of Use in all Ages and Countries. By F. W. FAIRHOLT, F.S.A. With upwards of 100 Illustrations by the Author. Crown 8vo, cloth extra, 6s.

Familiar Allusions : A Handbook of Miscellaneous Information; including the Names of Celebrated Statues, Paintings, Palaces, Country Seats, Ruins, Churches, Ships, Streets, Clubs, Natural Curiosities, and the like. By WILLIAM A. WHEELER, Author of " Noted Names of Fiction ; " and CHARLES G. WHEELER. Demy 8vo, cloth extra, 7s. 6d.

Familiar Short Sayings of Great Men. By SAMUEL ARTHUR BENT, A.M. Fifth Edition, Revised and Enlarged. Crown 6vo, cloth extra, 7s. 6d.

Farrer (James Anson), Works by:
Military Manners and Customs. Crown 8vo, cloth extra, 6s.
War: Three Essays, Reprinted from "Military Manners." Crown 8vo, 1s ; cloth, 1s. 6d.

Faraday (Michael), Works by :
Post 8vo, cloth extra, 4s. 6d. each.
The Chemical History of a Candle : Lectures delivered before a Juvenile Audience at the Royal Institution. Edited by WILLIAM CROOKES, F.C.S. With numerous Illustrations.
On the Various Forces of Nature, and their Relations to each other : Lectures delivered before a Juvenile Audience at the Royal Institution. Edited by WILLIAM CROOKES, F.C.S. With numerous Illustrations.

Fin-Bec. — The Cupboard Papers : Observations on the Art of Living and Dining. By FIN-BEC. Post 8vo, cloth limp, 2s. 6d.

Fireworks, The Complete Art of Making; or, The Pyrotechnist's Treasury. By THOMAS KENTISH. With 267 Illustrations. A New Edition, Revised throughout and greatly Enlarged. Crown 8vo, cloth extra, 5s.

Fitzgerald (Percy), Works by :
The Recreations of a Literary Man; or, Does Writing Pay ? With Recollections of some Literary Men, and a View of a Literary Man's Working Life. Cr. 8vo, cloth extra, 6s.
The World Behind the Scenes. Crown 8vo, cloth extra, 3s. 6d.
Little Essays: Passages from the Letters of CHARLES LAMB. Post 8vo, cloth limp. 2s. 6d.
Fatal Zero: A Homburg Diary. Cr. 8vo, cloth extra, 3s. 6d.

Post 8vo, illustrated boards, 2s. each.
Bella Donna. | Never Forgotten
The Second Mrs. Tillotson.
Polly.
Seventy-five Brooke Street.
The Lady of Brantome.

Fletcher's (Giles, B.D.) Complete Poems : Christ's Victorie in Heaven, Christ's Victorie on Earth, Christ's Triumph over Death, and Minor Poems. With Memorial-Introduction and Notes by the Rev. A. B. GROSART, D.D. Cr. 8vo, cloth bds., 6s.

Fonblanque.—Filthy Lucre : A Novel. By ALBANY DE FONBLANQUE. Post 8vo, illustrated boards, 2s.

Francillon (R. E.), Novels by :
Crown 8vo, cloth extra, 3s. 6d. each; post 8vo, illust. boards, 2s. each.
One by One. | A Real Queen.
Queen Cophetua. |

Olympia. Post 8vo, illust. boards, 2s.
Esther's Glove. Fcap. 8vo, 1s.

French Literature, History of.
By HENRY VAN LAUN. Complete in 3 Vols., demy 8vo, cl. bds., 7s. 6d. each.

Frere.—Pandurang Hari ; or, Memoirs of a Hindoo. With a Preface by Sir H. BARTLE FRERE, G.C.S.I., &c. Crown 8vo, cloth extra, 3s. 6d.; post 8vo, illustrated boards, 2s.

Friswell.—One of Two: A Novel. By HAIN FRISWELL. Post 8vo, illus- trated boards, 2s.

Frost (Thomas), Works by :
Crown 8vo, cloth extra, 3s. 6d. each.
Circus Life and Circus Celebrities.
The Lives of the Conjurers.
The Old Showmen and the Old London Fairs.

Fry's (Herbert) Royal Guide to the London Charities, 1886-7. Showing their Name, Date of Founda- tion,Objects,Income,Officials,&c. Pub- lished Annually. Cr. 8vo, cloth, 1s. 6d.

Gardening Books :
Post 8vo, 1s. each ; cl. limp, 1s. 6d. each.
A Year's Work in Garden and Green- house : Practical Advice to Amateur Gardeners as to the Management of the Flower,Fruit, and Frame Garden. By GEORGE GLENNY.
Our Kitchen Garden : The Plants we Grow, and How we Cook Them. By TOM JERROLD.
Household Horticulture: A Gossip about Flowers. By TOM and JANE JERROLD. Illustrated.
The Garden that Paid the Rent. By TOM JERROLD.

My Garden Wild, and What I Grew there. By F. G. HEATH. Crown 8vo, cloth extra, 5s.; gilt edges, 6s.

Garrett.—The Capel Girls : A Novel. By EDWARD GARRETT. Cr. 8vo, cl. ex., 3s. 6d. ; post 8vo, illust. bds., 2s.

Gentleman's Magazine (The) for 1887. One Shilling Monthly. In addition to the Articles upon subjects in Literature, Science, and Art, for which this Magazine has so high a reputation, "Science Notes," by W. MATTIEU WILLIAMS, F.R.A.S., and "Table Talk," by SYLVANUS URBAN, appear monthly.
** *Now ready, the Volume for* JANUARY to JUNE, 1887, *cloth extra, price* 8s. 6d.; *Cases for binding,* 2s. *each.*

German Popular Stories. Col- lected by the Brothers GRIMM, and Translated by EDGAR TAYLOR. Edited, with an Introduction, by JOHN RUSKIN. With 22 Illustrations on Steel by GEORGE CRUIKSHANK. Square 8vo, cloth extra, 6s. 6d. ; gilt edges, 7s. 6d.

Gibbon (Charles), Novels by :
Crown 8vo, cloth extra, 3s. 6d. each
post 8vo, illustrated boards, 2s. each.

Robin Gray.	The Flower of the
For Lack of Gold.	Forest. [lem.
What will the	A Heart's Prob-
World Say ?	The GoldenShaft.
In Honour Bound.	Of High Degree.
Queen of the	Fancy Free.
Meadow.	Loving a Dream.
Braes of Yarrow.	A Hard Knot.

Post 8vo, illustrated boards, 2s. each.
For the King. | In Pastures Green.
In Love and War.
By Mead and Stream.
Heart's Delight.   [*Preparing.*

Gilbert (William), Novels by :
Post 8vo, illustrated boards, 2s. each.
Dr. Austin's Guests.
The Wizard of the Mountain.
James Duke, Costermonger.

Gilbert (W. S.), Original Plays by: In Two Series, each complete in itself, price 2s. 6d. each.
The FIRST SERIES contains — The Wicked World—Pygmalion and Ga- latea — Charity — The Princess — The Palace of Truth—Trial by Jury.
The SECOND SERIES contains—Bro- ken Hearts—Engaged—Sweethearts— Gretchen—Dan'l Druce—Tom Cobb— H.M.S. Pinafore—The Sorcerer—The Pirates of Penzance.

Eight Original Comic Operas. Writ- ten by W. S. GILBERT. Containing: The Sorcerer—H.M.S. "Pinafore" —The Pirates of Penzance—Iolanthe — Patience — Princess Ida — The Mikado—Trial by Jury. Demy 8vo, cloth limp, 2s. 6d.

Glenny.—A Year's Work in Garden and Greenhouse : Practical Advice to Amateur Gardeners as to the Management of the Flower, Fruit, and Frame Garden. By GEORGE GLENNY. Post 8vo, 1s.; cloth, 1s. 6d.

Godwin.—Lives of the Necro- mancers. By WILLIAM GODWIN. Post 8vo, limp, 2s.

Golden Library, The:

Square 16mo (Tauchnitz size), cloth limp, 2s. per volume.

Bayard Taylor's Diversions of the Echo Club.

Bennett's (Dr. W. C.) Ballad History of England.

Bennett's (Dr.) Songs for Sailors.

Byron's Don Juan.

Godwin's (William) Lives of the Necromancers.

Holmes's Autocrat of the Breakfast Table. Introduction by SALA.

Holmes's Professor at the Breakfast Table.

Hood's Whims and Oddities. Complete. All the original Illustrations.

Irving's (Washington) Tales of a Traveller.

Jesse's (Edward) Scenes and Occupations of a Country Life.

Lamb's Essays of Elia. Both Series Complete in One Vol.

Leigh Hunt's Essays: A Tale for a Chimney Corner, and other Pieces. With Portrait, and Introduction by EDMUND OLLIER.

Mallory's (Sir Thomas) Mort d'Arthur: The Stories of King Arthur and of the Knights of the Round Table. Edited by B. MONTGOMERIE RANKING.

Pascal's Provincial Letters. A New Translation, with Historical Introduction and Notes, by T.M'CRIE,D.D.

Pope's Poetical Works. Complete.

Rochefoucauld's Maxims and Moral Reflections. With Notes, and Introductory Essay by SAINTE-BEUVE.

St. Pierre's Paul and Virginia, and The Indian Cottage. Edited, with Life, by the Rev. E. CLARKE.

Golden Treasury of Thought,

The: An ENCYCLOPÆDIA OF QUOTATIONS from Writers of all Times and Countries. Selected and Edited by THEODORE TAYLOR. Crown 8vo, cloth gilt and gilt edges, 7s. 6d.

Graham. — The Professor's

Wife: A Story. By LEONARD GRAHAM. Fcap. 8vo, picture cover, 1s.

Greeks and Romans, The Life

of the, Described from Antique Monuments. By ERNST GUHL and W. KONER. Translated from the Third German Edition, and Edited by Dr. F. HUEFFER. 545 Illusts. New and Cheaper Edit., demy 8vo, cl. ex., 7s. 6d.

Greenaway (Kate) and Bret

Harte.—The Queen of the Pirate Isle. By BRET HARTE. With 25 original Drawings by KATE GREENAWAY, Reproduced in Colours by E. EVANS. Sm. 4to, bds., 5s.

Greenwood (James),Works by:

Crown 8vo, cloth extra, 3s. 6d. each.

The Wilds of London.

Low-Life Deeps: An Account of the Strange Fish to be Found There.

Dick Temple: A Novel. Post 8vo, illustrated boards, 2s.

Guyot.—The Earth and Man;

or, Physical Geography in its relation to the History of Mankind. By ARNOLD GUYOT. With Additions by Professors AGASSIZ, PIERCE, and GRAY; 12 Maps and Engravings on Steel, some Coloured, and copious Index. Crown 8vo, cloth extra, gilt, 4s. 6d.

Habberton—Brueton's Bayou.

By JOHN HABBERTON, Author of "Helen's Babies." Post 8vo, illustrated boards, 2s.; cloth, 2s. 6d.

Hair (The): Its Treatment in

Health, Weakness, and Disease. Translated from the German of Dr. J. PINCUS. Crown 8vo, 1s.; cloth, 1s. 6d.

Hake (Dr. Thomas Gordon),

Poems by:

Crown 8vo, cloth extra, 6s. each.

New Symbols.

Legends of the Morrow.

The Serpent Play.

Maiden Ecstasy. Small 4to, cloth extra, 8s.

Hall.—Sketches of Irish Cha-

racter. By Mrs. S. C. HALL. With numerous Illustrations on Steel and Wood by MACLISE, GILBERT, HARVEY, and G. CRUIKSHANK. Medium 8vo, cloth extra, gilt, 7s. 6d.

Halliday.—Every-day Papers.

By ANDREW HALLIDAY. Post 8vo, illustrated boards, 2s.

Handwriting, The Philosophy

of. With over 100 Facsimiles and Explanatory Text. By DON FELIX DE SALAMANCA. Post 8vo, cl. limp, 2s.6d.

Hanky-Panky: A Collection of

Very EasyTricks,Very Difficult Tricks, White Magic, Sleight of Hand, &c. Edited by W. H. CREMER. With 200 Illusts. Crown 8vo, cloth extra, 4s. 6d.

Hardy (Lady Duffus). — Paul
Wynter's Sacrifice: A Story. By
Lady DUFFUS HARDY. Post 8vo, illust.
boards, 2s.

Hardy (Thomas).—Under the
Greenwood Tree. By THOMAS HARDY,
Author of "Far from the Madding
Crowd." With numerous Illustrations.
Crown 8vo, cloth extra, 3s. 6d.; post
8vo, illustrated boards, 2s.

Harwood.—The Tenth Earl.
By J. BERWICK HARWOOD. Post 8vo,
illustrated boards, 2s.

Haweis (Mrs. H. R.), Works by:
The Art of Dress. With numerous
Illustrations. Small 8vo, illustrated
cover, 1s.; cloth limp, 1s. 6d.

The Art of Beauty. New and Cheaper
Edition. Crown 8vo, cloth extra,
Coloured Frontispiece and Illusts.6s.

The Art of Decoration. Square 8vo,
handsomely bound and profusely
Illustrated, 10s. 6d.

Chaucer for Children: A Golden
Key. With Eight Coloured Pictures
and numerous Woodcuts. New
Edition, small 4to, cloth extra, 6s.

Chaucer for Schools. Demy 8vo,
cloth limp, 2s. 6d.

Haweis (Rev. H. R.).—American
Humorists. Including WASHINGTON
IRVING, OLIVER WENDELL HOLMES,
JAMES RUSSELL LOWELL, ARTEMUS
WARD, MARK TWAIN, and BRET HARTE.
By the Rev. H. R. HAWEIS, M.A.
Crown 8vo. cloth extra, 6s.

Hawthorne (Julian), Novels by.
Crown 8vo, cloth extra, 3s. 6d. each;
post 8vo, illustrated boards, 2s. each.

| Garth. | Sebastian Strome. |
| Ellice Quentin. | Dust. |

Prince Saroni's Wife.
Fortune's Fool. | Beatrix Randolph.

Crown 8vo, cloth extra, 3s. 6d. each.
Miss Cadogna.
Love—or a Name.

Mrs. Gainsborough's Diamonds.
Fcap. 8vo, illustrated cover, 1s.

Hays.—Women of the Day: A
Biographical Dictionary of Notable
Contemporaries. By FRANCES HAYS.
Crown 8vo, cloth extra, 5s.

Heath (F. G.). — My Garden
Wild, and What I Grew There. By
FRANCIS GEORGE HEATH, Author of
"The Fern World," &c. Crown 8vo,
cloth extra, 5s.; cl. gilt, gilt edges, 6s.

Helps (Sir Arthur), Works by:
Post 8vo, cloth limp, 2s. 6d. each.
Animals and their Masters.
Social Pressure.

Ivan de Biron: A Novel. Crown 8vo,
cloth extra, 3s. 6d.; post 8vo, illustrated boards, 2s.

Herrick's (Robert) Hesperides,
Noble Numbers, and Complete Collected Poems. With Memorial-Introduction and Notes by the Rev. A. B.
GROSART, D.D., Steel Portrait, Index
of First Lines, and Glossarial Index,
&c. Three Vols., crown 8vo, cloth, 18s.

Hesse - Wartegg   (Chevalier
Ernst von), Works by:
Tunis: The Land and the People.
With 22 Illustrations. Crown 8vo,
cloth extra, 3s. 6d.

The New South-West: Travelling
Sketches from Kansas, New Mexico,
Arizona, and Northern Mexico.
With 100 fine Illustrations and Three
Maps. Demy 8vo, cloth extra,
14s.   [In preparation.

Herbert.—The Poems of Lord
Herbert of Cherbury. Edited, with
Introduction, by J. CHURTON COLLINS.
Crown 8vo, bound in parchment, 8s.

Hindley (Charles), Works by:
Crown 8vo, cloth extra, 3s. 6d. each.
Tavern Anecdotes and Sayings: In-
cluding the Origin of Signs, and
Reminiscences connected with
Taverns, Coffee Houses, Clubs, &c.
With Illustrations.

The Life and Adventures of a Cheap
Jack. By One of the Fraternity.
Edited by CHARLES HINDLEY.

Hoey.—The Lover's Creed.
By Mrs. CASHEL HOEY. With Frontispiece by P. MACNAB. New and Cheaper
Edit. Crown 8vo, cloth extra, 3s. 6d.;
post 8vo, illustrated boards, 2s.

Holmes (O. Wendell), Works by:
The Autocrat of the Breakfast-
Table. Illustrated by J. GORDON
THOMSON. Post 8vo, cloth limp,
2s. 6d.—Another Edition in smaller
type, with an Introduction by G. A.
SALA. Post 8vo, cloth limp, 2s.

The Professor at the Breakfast
Table; with the Story of Iris. Post
8vo, cloth limp, 2s.

Holmes. — The Science of Voice Production and Voice Preservation: A Popular Manual for the Use of Speakers and Singers. By GORDON HOLMES, M.D. With Illustrations. Crown 8vo, 1s.; cloth, 1s. 6d.

Hood (Thomas):

Hood's Choice Works, in Prose and Verse. Including the Cream of the COMIC ANNUALS. With Life of the Author, Portrait, and 200 Illustrations. Crown 8vo, cloth extra, 7s. 6d.

Hood's Whims and Oddities. Complete. With all the original Illustrations. Post 8vo, cloth limp, 2s.

Hood (Tom), Works by:

From Nowhere to the North Pole: A Noah's Arkæological Narrative. With 25 Illustrations by W. BRUNTON and E. C. BARNES. Square crown 8vo, cloth extra, gilt edges, 6s.

A Golden Heart: A Novel. Post 8vo, illustrated boards, 2s.

Hook's (Theodore) Choice Humorous Works, including his Ludicrous Adventures, Bons Mots, Puns and Hoaxes. With a New Life of the Author, Portraits, Facsimiles, and Illusts. Cr. 8vo, cl. extra, gilt, 7s. 6d.

Hooper. — The House of Raby: A Novel. By Mrs. GEORGE HOOPER. Post 8vo, illustrated boards, 2s.

Hopkins — "'Twixt Love and Duty:" A Novel. By TIGHE HOPKINS. Crown 8vo, cloth extra, 6s.; post 8vo, illustrated boards, 2s.

Horne. — Orion : An Epic Poem, in Three Books. By RICHARD HENGIST HORNE. With Photographic Portrait from a Medallion by SUMMERS. Tenth Edition, crown 8vo, cloth extra, 7s.

Howell. — Conflicts of Capital and Labour, Historically and Economically considered : Being a History and Review of the Trade Unions of Great Britain. By GEO. HOWELL M.P. Crown 8vo, cloth extra, 7s. 6d.

Hunt. — Essays by Leigh Hunt. A Tale for a Chimney Corner, and other Pieces. With Portrait and Introduction by EDMUND OLLIER. Post 8vo, cloth limp, 2s.

Hunt (Mrs. Alfred), Novels by Crown 8vo, cloth extra, 3s. 6d. each. post 8vo, illustrated boards, 2s. each.

Thornicroft's Model.

The Leaden Casket.

Self-Condemned.

That other Person.

Indoor Paupers. By ONE OF THEM. Crown 8vo, 1s.; cloth, 1s. 6d.

Hydrophobia: M. PASTEUR'S System. Containing a Translation of all his Communications on the Subject, the Technique of his Methods, the latest Statistics, &c. By Dr. R. SUZOR. of the Faculties of Edinburgh and Paris. Cr. 8vo, cloth extra, 6s. [Shortly.

Ingelow. — Fated to be Free : A Novel. By JEAN INGELOW. Crown 8vo, cloth extra, 3s. 6d.; post 8vo, illustrated boards, 2s.

Irish Wit and Humour, Songs of. Collected and Edited by A. PERCEVAL GRAVES. Post 8vo, cloth limp, 2s. 6d.

Irving — Tales of a Traveller. By WASHINGTON IRVING. Post 8vo, cloth limp, 2s.

Jay (Harriett), Novels by:

The Dark Colleen. Post 8vo, illustrated boards, 2s.

The Queen of Connaught. Crown 8vo, cloth extra, 3s. 6d.; post 8vo, illustrated boards, 2s.

Janvier. — Practical Keramics for Students. By CATHERINE A. JANVIER. Crown 8vo, cloth extra, 6s.

Jefferies (Richard), Works by: Crown 8vo, cloth extra, 6s. each.

Nature near London.

The Life of the Fields.

The Open Air.

Jennings (H. J.), Works by:

Curiosities of Criticism. Post 8vo, cloth limp, 2s. 6d.

Lord Tennyson: A Biographical Sketch. With a Photograph-Portrait. Crown 8vo, cloth extra, 6s.

Jerrold (Tom), Works by :

Post 8vo, 1s. each ; cloth, 1s. 6d. each.

The Garden that Paid the Rent.

Household Horticulture: A Gossip about Flowers. Illustrated.

Our Kitchen Garden: The Plants we Grow, and How we Cook Them.

Jesse.—Scenes and Occupa-
tions of a Country Life. By EDWARD
JESSE. Post 8vo, cloth limp, 2s.

Jeux d'Esprit. Collected and
Edited by HENRY S. LEIGH. Post 8vo,
cloth limp, 2s. 6d.

Jones (Wm., F.S.A.), Works by:
Crown 8vo, cloth extra, 7s. 6d. each.

Finger-Ring Lore: Historical, Legendary, and Anecdotal. With over
Two Hundred Illustrations.

Credulities, Past and Present; in-
cluding the Sea and Seamen, Miners,
Talismans, Word and Letter Divina-
tion Exorcising and Blessing of
Animals, Birds, Eggs, Luck, &c.
With an Etched Frontispiece.

Crowns and Coronations: A History
of Regalia in all Times and Countries. With One Hundred Illustrations.

Jonson's (Ben) Works. With
Notes Critical and Explanatory, and
a Biographical Memoir by WILLIAM
GIFFORD. Edited by Colonel CUN-
NINGHAM. Three Vols., crown 8vo,
cloth extra, 18s.; or separately, 6s. each.

Josephus, The Complete Works
of. Translated by WHISTON. Containing both " The Antiquities of the
Jews " and " The Wars of the Jews."
Two Vols., 8vo, with 52 Illustrations
and Maps, cloth extra, gilt, 14s.

Kempt.—Pencil and Palette:
Chapters on Art and Artists. By ROBERT
KEMPT. Post 8vo, cloth limp, 2s 6d.

Kershaw.—Colonial Facts and
Fictions: Humorous Sketches. By
MARK KERSHAW. Post 8vo, illustrated
boards, 2s.; cloth, 2s. 6d.

King (R. Ashe), Novels by:
Crown 8vo, cloth extra, 3s. 6d. each;
post 8vo, illustrated boards, 2s. each.
A Drawn Game.
" The Wearing of the Green."

Kingsley (Henry), Novels by:
Oakshott Castle. Post 8vo, illustrated boards, 2s.
Number Seventeen. Crown 8vo, cloth
extra, 3s. 6d.

Knight.—The Patient's Vade
Mecum: How to get most Benefit
from Medical Advice. By WILLIAM
KNIGHT, M.R.C.S., and EDWARD
KNIGHT, L.R.C.P. Crown 8vo, 1s.;
cloth, 1s. 6d.

Lamb (Charles):
Lamb's Complete Works, in Prose
and Verse, reprinted from the Ori-
ginal Editions, with many Pieces
hitherto unpublished. Edited, with
Notes and Introduction, by R. H.
SHEPHERD. With Two Portraits and
Facsimile of Page of the " Essay on
Roast Pig." Crown 8vo, cloth extra,
7s. 6d.

The Essays of Elia. Complete Edition. Post 8vo, cloth extra, 2s.

Poetry for Children, and Prince
Dorus. By CHARLES LAMB. Care-
fully reprinted from unique copies.
Small 8vo, cloth extra, 5s.

Little Essays: Sketches and Characters. By CHARLES LAMB. Selected
from his Letters by PERCY FITZ-
GERALD. Post 8vo, cloth limp,
2s. 6d.

Lane's Arabian Nights, &c.:
The Thousand and One Nights:
commonly called, in England, " THE
ARABIAN NIGHTS' ENTERTAIN-
MENTS." A New Translation from
the Arabic, with copious Notes, by
EDWARD WILLIAM LANE. Illustrated
by many hundred Engravings on
Wood, from Original Designs by
WM. HARVEY. A New Edition, from
a Copy annotated by the Translator,
edited by his Nephew, EDWARD
STANLEY POOLE. With a Preface by
STANLEY LANE-POOLE. Three Vols.,
demy 8vo, cloth extra, 7s. 6d. each.

Arabian Society in the Middle Ages:
Studies from " The Thousand and
One Nights." By EDWARD WILLIAM
LANE, Author of " The Modern
Egyptians," &c. Edited by STANLEY
LANE-POOLE. Cr. 8vo, cloth extra, 6s.

Lares and Penates; or, The
Background of Life. By FLORENCE
CADDY. Crown 8vo, cloth extra, 6s.

Larwood (Jacob), Works by:
The Story of the London Parks.
With Illustrations. Crown 8vo, cloth
extra, 3s. 6d.

Post 8vo, cloth limp, 2s. 6d. each.
Forensic Anecdotes.
Theatrical Anecdotes.

Life in London; or, The History
of Jerry Hawthorn and Corinthian
Tom. With the whole of CRUIK-
SHANK'S Illustrations, in Colours, after
the Originals. Crown 8vo, cloth extra,
7s. 6d.

Linton (E. Lynn), Works by:
Post 8vo, cloth limp, 2s. 6d. each.

Witch Stories.

The True Story of Joshua Davidson.

Ourselves: Essays on Women.

Crown 8vo, cloth extra. 3s. 6d. each; post 8vo, illustrated boards, 2s. each.

Patricia Kemball.

The Atonement of Leam Dundas.

The World Well Lost.

Under which Lord?

With a Silken Thread.

The Rebel of the Family.

"My Love!" | Ione.

Longfellow:
Crown 8vo, cloth extra, 7s. 6d. each.

Longfellow's Complete Prose Works. Including "Outre Mer," "Hyperion," "Kavanagh," "The Poets and Poetry of Europe," and "Driftwood." With Portrait and Illustrations by VALENTINE BROMLEY.

Longfellow's Poetical Works. Carefully Reprinted from the Original Editions. With numerous fine Illustrations on Steel and Wood.

Long Life, Aids to: A Medical, Dietetic, and General Guide in Health and Disease. By N. E. DAVIES, L.R.C.P. Crown 8vo, 2s. ; cloth limp, 2s. 6d.

Lucy.—Gideon Fleyce: A Novel. By HENRY W. LUCY. Crown 8vo, cl. ex., 3s. 6d : post 8vo. illust. bds., 2s.

Lusiad (The) of Camoens. Translated into English Spenserian Verse by ROBERT FFRENCH DUFF. Demy 8vo, with Fourteen full-page Plates, cloth boards, 18s.

Macalpine. — Teresa Itasca, and other Stories. By AVERY MACALPINE. Crown 8vo, bound in canvas, 2s. 6d.

McCarthy (Justin, M.P.), Works by:
A History of Our Own Times, from the Accession of Queen Victoria to the General Election of 1880. Four Vols. demy 8vo, cloth extra, 12s. each.—Also a POPULAR EDITION, in Four Vols. cr. 8vo, cl. extra, 6s. each. —And a JUBILEE EDITION, with an Appendix of Events to the end of 1886, complete in Two Vols., square 8vo, cloth extra, 7s. 6d. each.

McCarthy (Justin), continued—
A Short History of Our Own Times. One Vol., crown 8vo, cloth extra, 6s.

History of the Four Georges. Four Vols. demy 8vo, cloth extra, 12s. each.   [Vol. I. now ready.

Crown 8vo, cloth extra, 3s. 6d. each; post 8vo, illustrated boards, 2s. each.

Dear Lady Disdain.

The Waterdale Neighbours.

My Enemy's Daughter.

A Fair Saxon.

Miss Misanthrope.

Donna Quixote.

The Comet of a Season.

Maid of Athens.

Camiola: A Girl with a Fortune.

Linley Rochford. Post 8vo, illustrated boards, 2s.

"The Right Honourable:" A Romance of Society and Politics. By JUSTIN McCARTHY, M.P., and Mrs. CAMPBELL-PRAED. New and Cheaper Edition, crown 8vo, cloth extra, 6s.

McCarthy (Justin H., M.P.), Works by:
An Outline of the History of Ireland, from the Earliest Times to the Present Day. Cr. 8vo, 1s. ; cloth, 1s. 6d.

Ireland since the Union: Sketches of Irish History from 1798 to 1886. Crown 8vo, cloth extra, 6s.

The Case for Home Rule. Crown 8vo, cloth extra, 6s.

England under Gladstone, 1880-85. Second Edition, revised. Crown 8vo, cloth extra, 6s.

Doom! An Atlantic Episode. Crown 8vo, 1s. ; cloth, 1s. 6d.

Our Sensation Novel. Edited by JUSTIN H. McCARTHY. Crown 8vo, 1s. ; cloth, 1s. 6d.

Hafiz in London. Choicely printed. Small 8vo, gold cloth, 3s. 6d.

Macdonell.—Quaker Cousins: A Novel. By AGNES MACDONELL. Crown 8vo, cloth extra, 3s. 6d.; post 8vo, illustrated boards, 2s.

Macgregor. — Pastimes and Players. Notes on Popular Games. By ROBERT MACGREGOR. Post 8vo, cloth limp, 2s. 6d.

Mackay.—Interludes and Undertones; or, Music at Twilight. By CHARLES MACKAY, LL.D. Crown 8vo, cloth extra, 6s.

MacDonald (George, LL.D.),
Works by :

Works of Fancy and Imagination.
Pocket Edition, Ten Volumes, in
handsome cloth case, 21s. Vol. 1.
WITHIN AND WITHOUT. THE HID-
DEN LIFE.—Vol. 2. THE DISCIPLE.
THE GOSPEL WOMEN. A BOOK OF
SONNETS. ORGAN SONGS.—Vol. 3.
VIOLIN SONGS. SONGS OF THE DAYS
AND NIGHTS. A BOOK OF DREAMS.
ROADSIDE POEMS. POEMS FOR
CHILDREN. Vol. 4. PARABLES.
BALLADS. SCOTCH SONGS.—Vols.
5 and 6. PHANTASTES: A Faerie
Romance.—Vol. 7. THE PORTENT.—
Vol. 8. THE LIGHT PRINCESS. THE
GIANT'S HEART. SHADOWS. — Vol.
9. CROSS PURPOSES. THE GOLDEN
KEY. THE CARASOYN. LITTLE
DAYLIGHT.— Vol. 10. THE CRUEL
PAINTER. THE WOW O' RIVVEN.
THE CASTLE. THE BROKEN SWORDS.
THE GRAY WOLF. UNCLE CORNE-
LIUS.

*The Volumes are also sold separately
in Grolier-pattern cloth,* 2s. 6d. *each.*

Maclise Portrait-Gallery (The)
of Illustrious Literary Characters;
with Memoirs—Biographical, Critical,
Bibliographical, and Anecdotal—illus-
trative of the Literature of the former
half of the Present Century. By
WILLIAM BATES, B.A. With 85 Portraits printed on an India Tint. Crown
8vo, cloth extra, 7s. 6d.

Macquoid (Mrs.), Works by :
Square 8vo, cloth extra, 10s. 6d. each.

In the Ardennes. With 50 fine Illustrations by THOMAS R. MACQUOID.

Pictures and Legends from Normandy and Brittany. With numerous Illustrations by THOMAS R.
MACQUOID.

About Yorkshire. With 67 Illustrations by T. R. MACQUOID.

Crown 8vo, cloth extra, 7s. 6d. each.

Through Normandy. With 90 Illustrations by T. R. MACQUOID.

Through Brittany. With numerous
Illustrations by T. R. MACQUOID.

Post 8vo, illustrated boards, 2s. each.

The Evil Eye, and other Stories.

Lost Rose.

Magician's Own Book (The) :
Performances with Cups and Balls,
Eggs, Hats, Handkerchiefs, &c. All
from actual Experience. Edited by
W. H. CREMER. With 200 Illustrations.
Crown 8vo, cloth extra, 4s. 6d.

Magic Lantern (The), and its
Management: including full Prac-
tical Directions for producing the
Limelight, making Oxygen Gas, and
preparing Lantern Slides. By T. C.
HEPWORTH. With 10 Illustrations.
Crown 8vo, 1s. ; cloth, 1s. 6d.

Magna Charta. An exact Fac-
simile of the Original in the British
Museum, printed on fine plate paper,
3 feet by 2 feet, with Arms and Seals
emblazoned in Gold and Colours. 5s.

Mallock (W. H.), Works by :
The New Republic; or, Culture, Faith
and Philosophy in an English Country
House. Post 8vo, cloth limp, 2s. 6d. ;
Cheap Edition, illustrated boards, 2s.

The New Paul and Virginia ; or, Posi-
tivism on an Island. Post 8vo, cloth
limp, 2s. 6d.

Poems. Small 4to, in parchment, 8s.

Is Life worth Living? Crown 8vo,
cloth extra, 6s.

Mallory's (Sir Thomas) Mort
d'Arthur: The Stories of King Arthur
and of the Knights of the Round Table.
Edited by B. MONTGOMERIE RANKING.
Post 8vo, cloth limp, 2s.

Mark Twain, Works by :
The Choice Works of Mark Twain.
Revised and Corrected throughout by
the Author. With Life, Portrait, and
numerous Illustrations. Crown 8vo,
cloth extra, 7s. 6d.

The Innocents Abroad ; or, The New
Pilgrim's Progress: Being some Account of the Steamship " Quaker
City's " Pleasure Excursion to
Europe and the Holy Land. With
234 Illustrations. Crown 8vo, cloth
extra, 7s. 6d.—Cheap Edition (under
the title of " MARK TWAIN'S PLEASURE
TRIP "), post 8vo, illust. boards, 2s.

Roughing It, and The Innocents at
Home. With 200 Illustrations by
F. A. FRASER. Crown 8vo, cloth
extra, 7s. 6d.

The Gilded Age. By MARK TWAIN
and CHARLES DUDLEY WARNER.
With 212 Illustrations by T COPPIN.
Crown 8vo, cloth extra, 7s. 6d.

The Adventures of Tom Sawyer.
With 111 Illustrations. Crown 8vo,
cloth extra, 7s. 6d.—Cheap Edition,
post 8vo, illustrated boards, 2s.

The Prince and the Pauper. With
nearly 200 Illustrations. Crown 8vo,
cloth extra, 7s. 6d.

MARK TWAIN'S WORKS, continued—

A Tramp Abroad. With 314 Illustrations. Crown 8vo, cloth extra, 7s. 6d. —Cheap Edition, post 8vo, illustrated boards, 2s.

The Stolen White Elephant, &c. Crown 8vo, cloth extra, 6s.; post 8vo, illustrated boards, 2s.

Life on the Mississippi. With about 300 Original Illustrations. Crown 8vo, cloth extra, 7s. 6d.—Cheap Edition, post 8vo, illustrated boards, 2s.

The Adventures of Huckleberry Finn. With 174 Illustrations by E. W. KEMBLE. Crown 8vo, cloth extra, 7s. 6d.—Cheap Edition, post 8vo, illustrated boards, 2s.

Marlowe's Works. Including his Translations. Edited, with Notes and Introductions, by Col. CUNNINGHAM. Crown 8vo, cloth extra, 6s.

Marryat (Florence), Novels by: Crown 8vo, cloth extra, 3s. 6d. each; post 8vo, illustrated boards, 2s. each.

Open! Sesame!
Written in Fire

Post 8vo, illustrated boards, 2s. each.

A Harvest of Wild Oats.
A Little Stepson.
Fighting the Air.

Massinger's Plays. From the Text of WILLIAM GIFFORD. Edited by Col. CUNNINGHAM. Crown 8vo, cloth extra, 6s.

Masterman.—Half a Dozen Daughters: A Novel. By J. MASTERMAN. Post 8vo, illustrated boards, 2s.

Matthews.—A Secret of the Sea, &c. By BRANDER MATTHEWS. Post 8vo, illustrated boards, 2s ; cloth, 2s. 6d.

Mayfair Library, The: Post 8vo, cloth limp, 2s. 6d. per Volume.

A Journey Round My Room. By XAVIER DE MAISTRE. Translated by HENRY ATTWELL.

Quips and Quiddities. Selected by W. DAVENPORT ADAMS.

The Agony Column of "The Times," from 1800 to 1870. Edited, with an Introduction, by ALICE CLAY.

Melancholy Anatomised: A Popular Abridgment of "Burton's Anatomy of Melancholy."

Gastronomy as a Fine Art. By BRILLAT-SAVARIN.

MAYFAIR LIBRARY, continued—

The Speeches of Charles Dickens.

Literary Frivolities, Fancies, Follies, and Frolics. By W. T. DOBSON.

Poetical Ingenuities and Eccentricities. Selected and Edited by W. T. DOBSON.

The Cupboard Papers. By FIN-BEC.

Original Plays by W. S. GILBERT. FIRST SERIES. Containing: The Wicked World — Pygmalion and Galatea— Charity — The Princess— The Palace of Truth—Trial by Jury.

Original Plays by W. S. GILBERT. SECOND SERIES. Containing: Broken Hearts — Engaged — Sweethearts— Gretchen—Dan'l Druce—Tom Cobb —H.M.S. Pinafore — The Sorcerer —The Pirates of Penzance.

Songs of Irish Wit and Humour. Collected and Edited by A. PERCEVAL GRAVES.

Animals and their Masters. By Sir ARTHUR HELPS.

Social Pressure. By Sir A. HELPS.

Curiosities of Criticism. By HENRY J. JENNINGS.

The Autocrat of the Breakfast-Table. By OLIVER WENDELL HOLMES. Illustrated by J. GORDON THOMSON.

Pencil and Palette. By ROBERT KEMPT.

Little Essays: Sketches and Characters. By CHAS. LAMB. Selected from his Letters by PERCY FITZGERALD.

Forensic Anecdotes; or, Humour and Curiosities of the Law and Men of Law. By JACOB LARWOOD.

Theatrical Anecdotes. By JACOB LARWOOD.

Jeux d'Esprit. Edited by HENRY S. LEIGH.

True History of Joshua Davidson. By E. LYNN LINTON.

Witch Stories. By E. LYNN LINTON.

Ourselves: Essays on Women. By E. LYNN LINTON.

Pastimes and Players. By ROBERT MACGREGOR.

The New Paul and Virginia. By W. H. MALLOCK.

New Republic. By W. H. MALLOCK.

Puck on Pegasus. By H. CHOLMONDELEY-PENNELL.

Pegasus Re-Saddled. By H. CHOLMONDELEY-PENNELL. Illustrated by GEORGE DU MAURIER.

Muses of Mayfair. Edited by H. CHOLMONDELEY-PENNELL.

Thoreau: His Life and Aims. By H. A. PAGE.

MAYFAIR LIBRARY, *continued.* .

Puniana. By the Hon. HUGH ROWLEY.

More Puniana. By the Hon. HUGH ROWLEY.

The Philosophy of Handwriting. By DON FELIX DE SALAMANCA.

By Stream and Sea. By WILLIAM SENIOR.

Old Stories Re-told. By WALTER THORNBURY.

Leaves from a Naturalist's Note-Book. By Dr. ANDREW WILSON.

Mayhew.—London Characters and the Humorous Side of London Life. By HENRY MAYHEW. With numerous Illustrations. Crown 8vo, cloth extra, 3s. 6d.

Medicine, Family.—One Thou-sand Medical Maxims and Surgical Hints, for Infancy, Adult Life, Middle Age, and Old Age. By N. E. DAVIES, L.R.C.P Lond   Cr. 8vo, 1s.; cl., 1s. 6d.

Merry Circle (The): A Book of New Intellectual Games and Amusements. By CLARA BELLEW. With numerous Illustrations. Crown 8vo, cloth extra, 4s. 6d.

Mexican Mustang (On a), through Texas, from the Gulf to the Rio Grande. A New Book of American Humour. By ALEX. E. SWEET and J. ARMOY KNOX, Editors of "Texas Siftings" With 265 Illusts. Cr. 8vo, cloth extra, 7s. 6d.

Middlemass (Jean), Novels by: Post 8vo, illustrated boards 2s. each. Touch and Go. | Mr. Dorillion.

Miller.—Physiology for the Young; or, The House of Life: Human Physiology, with its application to the Preservation of Health. For Classes and Popular Reading. With numerous Illusts. By Mrs. F. FENWICK MILLER. Small 8vo, cloth limp, 2s. 6d.

Milton (J. L.), Works by: Sm. 8vo, 1s. each ; cloth ex., 1s. 6d. each.

The Hygiene of the Skin. A Concise Set of Rules for the Management of the Skin; with Directions for Diet, Wines. Soaps, Baths, &c.

The Bath in Diseases of the Skin.

The Laws of Life, and their Relation to Diseases of the Skin.

Molesworth (Mrs.).—Hather-court Rectory. By Mrs. MOLESWORTH, Author of "The Cuckoo Clock," &c. Crown 8vo, cloth extra, 4s. 6d.

Moncrieff.—The Abdication; or, Time Tries All.   An Historical Drama. By W. D. SCOTT-MONCRIEFF. With Seven Etchings by JOHN PETTIE, R.A., W. Q. ORCHARDSON, R.A., J. MACWHIRTER, A.R.A.,COLIN HUNTER, A.R.A., R. MACBETH. A R.A , and TOM GRAHAM, R.S.A.   Large 4to, bound in buckram, 21s.

Murray (D. Christie), Novels by. Crown 8vo,cloth extra. 3s. 6d. each ; post 8vo, illustrated boards, 2s. each.

A Life's Atonement.|A Model Father.

Joseph's Coat. |Coals of Fire.

By the Gate of the Sea.

Val Strange. |Hearts.

The Way of the World.

A Bit of Human Nature.

First Person Singular.

Cynic Fortune.

Old Blazer's Hero.   With Illustrations by A. MCCORMICK. Two Vols., post 8vo. 12s.   [*Shortly.*

North Italian Folk. By Mrs. COMYNS CARR.   Illustrated by RANDOLPH CALDECOTT.   Square 8vo, cloth extra, 7s. 6d.

Nursery Hints: A Mother's Guide in Health and Disease. By N. E. DAVIES, L.R.C.P. Crown 8vo, 1s.; cloth, 1s. 6d.

O'Connor.—Lord Beaconsfield A Biography. By T. P. O'CONNOR, M.P. Sixth Edition, with a New Preface, bringing the work down to the Death of Lord Beaconsfield. Crown 8vo, cloth extra, 7s. 6d.

O'Hanlon. — The Unforeseen : A Novel. By ALICE O'HANLON. New and Cheaper Edition. Post 8vo, illustrated boards, 2s.

Oliphant (Mrs.) Novels by : Whiteladies. With Illustrations by ARTHUR HOPKINS and H. Woons. Crown 8vo, cloth extra, 3s. 6d. ; post 8vo, illustrated boards, 2s.

Crown 8vo, cloth extra, 4s. 6d. each. The Primrose Path. The Greatest Heiress in England.

O'Reilly.—Phœbe's Fortunes : A Novel. With Illustrations by HENRY TUCK. Post 8vo, illustrated boards, 2s.

O'Shaughnessy (Arth.), Works by : Songs of a Worker. Fcap. 8vo, cloth extra, 7s. 6d.

Music and Moonlight. Fcap. 8vo, cloth extra. 7s. 6d.

Lays of France. Crown 8vo, cloth extra, 10s. 6d.

Ouida, Novels by. Crown 8vo,
cloth extra, 5s. each; post 8vo, illustrated boards, 2s. each.

Held In Bondage.	Signa.
Strathmore.	In a Winter City.
Chandos.	Ariadne
Under Two Flags.	Friendship.
Cecil Castle-	Moths.
maine's Gage.	Pipistrello.
Idalia	A Village Com-
Tricotrin.	mune.
Puck.	Bimbi.
Folle Farine.	In Maremma
TwoLittleWooden	Wanda.
Shoes.	Frescoes. [Ine.
A Dog of Flanders	Princess Naprax-
Pascarel.	Othmar.

Wisdom, Wit, and Pathos, selected from the Works of OUIDA by F. SYDNEY MORRIS. Sm.cr.8vo,cl.ex.,5s.

Page (H. A.), Works by :
Thoreau: His Life and Aims: A Study. With Portrait. Post 8vo,cl.limp,2s.6d.
Lights on the Way: Some Tales within a Tale. By the late J. H. ALEXANDER, B.A. Edited by H. A. PAGE. Crown 8vo, cloth extra, 6s.
Animal Anecdotes. Arranged on a New Principle. Cr. 8vo, cl. extra, 5s.

Parliamentary Elections and
Electioneering in the Old Days (A History of). Showing the State of Political Parties and Party Warfare at the Hustings and in the House of Commons from the Stuarts to Queen Victoria. Illustrated from the original Political Squibs, Lampoons, Pictorial Satires, and Popular Caricatures of the Time. By JOSEPH GREGO, Author of "Rowlandson and his Works," "The Life of Gillray," &c. Demy 8vo, cloth extra, with a Frontispiece coloured by hand, and nearly 100 Illustrations, 16s.

Pascal's Provincial Letters. A
New Translation, with Historical Introduction and Notes, by T. M'CRIE, D.D. Post 8vo, cloth limp, 2s.

Patient's (The) Vade Mecum :
How to get most Benefit from Medical Advice. By WILLIAM KNIGHT, M.R.C.S., and EDWARD KNIGHT, L.R.C.P. Crown 8vo, 1s.; cloth, 1s.6d.

Paul Ferroll :
Post 8vo, illustrated boards, 2s. each.
Paul Ferroll: A Novel.
Why Paul Ferroll Killed his Wife.

Paul.—Gentle and Simple. By
MARGARET AGNES PAUL. With a Frontispiece by HELEN PATERSON. Cr. 8vo, cloth extra. 3s. 6d. ; post 8vo, illustrated boards, 2s.

Payn (James), Novels by.
Crown 8vo, cloth extra. 3s. 6d. each; post 8vo, illustrated boards, 2s. each.
Lost Sir Massingberd.
The Best of Husbands.
Walter's Word. | Halves.
What He Cost Her.
Less Black than we're Painted.
By Proxy. | High Spirits.
Under One Roof.
A Confidential Agent.
Some Private Views.
A Grape from a Thorn.
For Cash Only. | From Exile.
The Canon's Ward.
Post 8vo, illustrated boards, 2s. each.
Kit: A Memory. | Carlyon's Year.
A Perfect Treasure.
Bentinck's Tutor.|Murphy's Master.
Fallen Fortunes.
A County Family.|At Her Mercy.
A Woman's Vengeance.
Cecil's Tryst.
The Clyffards of Clyffe.
The Family Scapegrace.
The Foster Brothers.|Found Dead.
Gwendoline's Harvest.
Humorous Stories.
Like Father, Like Son.
A Marine Residence.
Married Beneath Him.
Mirk Abbey.| Not Wooed, but Won.
Two Hundred Pounds Reward.
The Talk of the Town.
In Peril and Privation: Stories of Marine Adventure Re-told. A Book for Boys. With numerous Illustrations. Crown 8vo, cloth gilt, 6s.
Holiday Tasks: Being Essays written in Vacation Time. Crown 8vo, cloth extra, 6s.
Glow-Worm Tales. Three Vols., crown 8vo.

Pears.—The Present Depres-
sion in Trade: Its Causes and Remedies. Being the "Pears" Prize Essays (of One Hundred Guineas). By EDWIN GOADBY and WILLIAM WATT. With an Introductory Paper by Prof. LEONE LEVI, F.S.A., F.S S. Demy 8vo, 1s.

Pennell (H. Cholmondeley),
Works by :
Post 8vo, cloth limp. 2s. 6d. each.
Puck on Pegasus. With Illustrations.
Pegasus Re-Saddled. With Ten full-page Illusts. by G. DU MAURIER.
The Muses of Mayfair. Vers de Société, Selected and Edited by H. C. PENNELL.

Phelps (E. Stuart), Works by:
Post 8vo. 1s. each; cl. limp, 1s. 6d. each.
Beyond the Gates. By the Author of "The Gates Ajar."
An Old Maid's Paradise.
Burglars in Paradise.

Pirkis (Mrs. C. L.), Novels by:
Trooping with Crows. Fcap. 8vo, picture cover, 1s.
Lady Lovelace. Post 8vo, illustrated boards, 2s.   [*Preparing.*

Planché (J. R.), Works by:
The Pursuivant of Arms; or, Heraldry Founded upon Facts. With Coloured Frontispiece and 200 Illustrations. Cr. 8vo, cloth extra, 7s. 6d.
Songs and Poems, from 1819 to 1879. Edited, with an Introduction, by his Daughter, Mrs. Mackarness. Crown 8vo, cloth extra, 6s.

Plutarch's Lives of Illustrious Men. Translated from the Greek, with Notes Critical and Historical, and a Life of Plutarch, by John and William Langhorne. Two Vols., 8vo, cloth extra, with Portraits, 10s. 6d.

Poe (Edgar Allan):—
The Choice Works, in Prose and Poetry, of Edgar Allan Poe. With an Introductory Essay by Charles Baudelaire, Portrait and Facsimiles. Crown 8vo, cl. extra, 7s. 6d.
The Mystery of Marie Roget, and other Stories. Post 8vo. illust.bds.,2s.

Pope's Poetical Works. Complete in One Vol. Post 8vo, cl. limp, 2s.

Praed (Mrs. Campbell-).—"The Right Honourable:" A Romance of Society and Politics. By Mrs. Campbell-Praed and Justin McCarthy, M.P. Cr. 8vo, cloth extra, 6s.

Princess Olga—Radna; or, The Great Conspiracy of 1831. By the Princess Olga. Cr. 8vo, cl. ex., 6s.

Proctor (Richd. A.), Works by:
Flowers of the Sky. With 55 Illusts. Small crown 8vo, cloth extra, 4s. 6d.
Easy Star Lessons. With Star Maps for Every Night in the Year, Drawings of the Constellations, &c. Crown 8vo, cloth extra, 6s.
Familiar Science Studies. Crown 8vo, cloth extra, 7s. 6d.
Saturn and Its System. New and Revised Edition, with 13 Steel Plates. Demy 8vo, cloth extra, 10s. 6d.
The Great Pyramid: Observatory, Tomb, and Temple. With Illustrations. Crown 8vo, cloth extra, 6s.
Mysteries of Time and Space. With Illusts. Cr. 8vo. cloth extra, 7s. 6d.
The Universe of Suns, and other Science Gleanings. With numerous Illusts. Cr. 8vo, cloth extra, 7s. 6d.
Wages and Wants of Science Workers. Crown 8vo, 1s. 6d.

Price (E. C.), Novels by:
Crown 8vo, cloth extra, 3s. 6d. each; post 8vo, illustrated boards, 2s. each.
Valentina. | The Foreigners.
Mrs. Lancaster's Rival.
Gerald. Post 8vo, illust. boards, 2s.

Rabelais' Works. Faithfully Translated from the French, with variorum Notes, and numerous characteristic Illustrations by Gustave Doré. Crown 8vo, cloth extra, 7s. 6d.

Rambosson.—Popular Astronomy. By J. Rambosson, Laureate of the Institute of France. Translated by C. B. Pitman. Crown 8vo, cloth gilt, numerous Illusts., and a beautifully executed Chart of Spectra, 7s. 6d.

Reade (Charles), Novels by:
Cr. 8vo, cloth extra, illustrated,3s.6d. each; post 8vo, illust. bds., 2s. each.
Peg Woffington. Illustrated by S. L. Fildes, A R.A.
Christie Johnstone. Illustrated by William Small.
It Is Never Too Late to Mend. Illustrated by G. J. Pinwell.
The Course of True Love Never did run Smooth. Illustrated by Helen Paterson.
The Autobiography of a Thief; Jack of all Trades; and James Lambert. Illustrated by Matt Stretch.
Love me Little, Love me Long. Illustrated by M. Ellen Edwards.
The Double Marriage. Illust. by Sir John Gilbert, R.A., and C. Keene.
The Cloister and the Hearth. Illustrated by Charles Keene.
Hard Cash. Illust. by F. W. Lawson.
Griffith Gaunt. Illustrated by S. L. Fildes, A.R.A., and Wm. Small.
Foul Play. Illust. by Du Maurier.
Put Yourself in His Place. Illustrated by Robert Barnes.
A Terrible Temptation. Illustrated by Edw. Hughes and A. W. Cooper.
The Wandering Heir. Illustrated by H. Paterson, S. L. Fildes, A.R.A., C. Green, and H. Woods, A.R A.
A Simpleton. Illustrated by Kate Crauford.
A Woman-Hater. Illustrated by Thos Couldery.
Singleheart and Doubleface: A Matter-of-fact Romance. Illustrated by P. Macnab.
Good Stories of Men and other Animals. Illustrated by E. A. Abbey, Percy Macquoid, and Joseph Nash.
The Jilt, and other Stories. Illustrated by Joseph Nash.
Readiana. With a Steel-plate Portrait of Charles Reade.

Reader's Handbook (The) of
Allusions, References, Plots, and
Stories. By the Rev. Dr. BREWER.
Fifth Edition, revised throughout,
with a New Appendix, containing a
COMPLETE ENGLISH BIBLIOGRAPHY.
Cr. 8vo, 1,400 pages, cloth extra, 7s. 6d.

Red Spider: A Romance. By
the Author of "John Herring," &c.
Two Vols., crown 8vo.

Richardson. — A Ministry of
Health, and other Papers. By BEN-
JAMIN WARD RICHARDSON, M.D., &c.
Crown 8vo, cloth extra, 6s.

Riddell (Mrs. J. H.), Novels by:
Crown 8vo, cloth extra, 3s. 6d. each;
post 8vo, illustrated boards, 2s. each.
Her Mother's Darling.
The Prince of Wales's Garden Party
Weird Stories.

Post 8vo, illustrated boards, 2s. each.
The Uninhabited House.
Fairy Water.
The Mystery In Palace Gardens.

Rimmer (Alfred), Works by:
Square 8vo, cloth gilt, 10s 6d each.
Our Old Country Towns. With over
50 Illustrations.
Rambles Round Eton and Harrow.
With 50 Illustrations.
About England with Dickens. With
58 Illustrations by ALFRED RIMMER
and C. A. VANDERHOOF.

Robinson Crusoe: A beautiful
reproduction of Major's Edition, with
37 Woodcuts and Two Steel Plates by
GEORGE CRUIKSHANK, choicely printed.
Crown 8vo, cloth extra, 7s. 6d.

Robinson (F. W.), Novels by:
Crown 8vo, cloth extra, 3s. 6d. each;
post 8vo, illustrated boards, 2s. each.
Women are Strange.
The Hands of Justice.

Robinson (Phil), Works by:
Crown 8vo, cloth extra, 7s. 6d. each.
The Poets' Birds.
The Poets' Beasts.
The Poets and Nature: Reptiles,
Fishes and Insects. [*Preparing.*

Rochefoucauld's Maxims and
Moral Reflections. With Notes, and
an Introductory Essay by SAINTE-
BEUVE. Post 8vo, cloth limp, 2s.

Roll of Battle Abbey, The; or,
A List of the Principal Warriors who
came over from Normandy with William the Conqueror, and Settled in
this Country, A.D. 1066-7. With the
principal Arms emblazoned in Gold
and Colours. Handsomely printed, 5s.

Rowley (Hon. Hugh), Works by:
Post 8vo, cloth limp, 2s. 6d. each.
Puniana: Riddles and Jokes. With
numerous Illustrations.
More Puniana. Profusely Illustrated.

Runciman (James), Stories by
Post 8vo, illustrated boards, 2s. each
cloth limp, 2s. 6d each.
Skippers and Shellbacks.
Grace Balmaign's Sweetheart.
Schools and Scholars.

Russell (W. Clark), Works by:
Crown 8vo, cloth extra, 6s each; post
8vo, illustrated boards, 2s. each.,
Round the Galley-Fire.
On the Fo'k'sle Head: A Collection
of Yarns and Sea Descriptions.
In the Middle Watch.

Crown 8vo, cloth extra, 6s. each.
A Voyage to the Cape.
A Book for the Hammock.[*Preparing.*
The Frozen Pirate. The New Serial
Nove: by W. CLARK RUSSELL, Author
of "The Wreck of the *Grosvenor*,"
begins in "Belgravia" for July, and
will be continued till January next.
One Shilling, Monthly. Illustrated.

Sala.—Gaslight and Daylight.
By GEORGE AUGUSTUS SALA. Post
8vo, illustrated boards. 2s.

Sanson.—Seven Generations
of Executioners: Memoirs of the
Sanson Family (1688 to 1847). Edited
by HENRY SANSON. Cr.8vo,cl.ex.3s 6d.

Saunders (John), Novels by:
Crown 8vo, cloth extra, 3s. 6d. each;
post 8vo, illustrated boards, 2s. each.
Bound to the Wheel
Guy Waterman.|Lion in the Path.
The Two Dreamers.
One Against the World. Post 8vo,
illustrated boards, 2s.

Saunders (Katharine), Novels
by. Cr. 8vo, cloth extra, 3s. 6d. each;
post 8vo, illustrated boards, 2s. each.
Joan Merryweather.
Margaret and Elizabeth.
The High Mills.
Heart Salvage. | Sebastian.
Gideon's Rock.
Crown 8vo, cloth extra, 3s. 6d.

Science Gossip: An Illustrated
Medium of Interchange for Students
and Lovers of Nature. Edited by J. E.
TAYLOR, F.L.S., &c. Devoted to Geo-
logy, Botany, Physiology, Chemistry,
Zoology, Microscopy, Telescopy, Phy-
siography, &c. Price 4d. Monthly; or
5s per year, post free. Vols. I. to
XIV. may be had at 7s. 6d. each; and
Vols. XV. to XXII. (1886), at 5s. each.
Cases for Binding, 1s. 6d. each.

Scott (Sir Walter), Poems by :

Marmion. With over 100 new Illusts. by leading Artists. Sm.4to,cl.ex 16s.

The Lay of the Last Minstrel. With over 100 new Illustrations by leading Artists. Sm. 4to, cl. ex., 16s.

"Secret Out" Series, The : Cr. 8vo, cl. ex., Illusts., 4s. 6d. each.

The Secret Out: One Thousand Tricks with Cards, and other Recreations; with Entertaining Experiments in Drawing-room or " White Magic." By W. H.CREMER. 300Illusts.

The Art of Amusing: A Collection of Graceful Arts,Games,Tricks,Puzzles, and Charades By FRANK BELLEW. With 300 Illustrations.

Hanky-Panky: Very Easy Tricks, Very Difficult Tricks, White Magic Sleight of Hand. Edited by W. H. CREMER. With 200 Illustrations.

The Merry Circle: A Book of New Intellectual Games and Amusements. By CLARA BELLEW. Many Illusts.

Magician's Own Book: Performances with Cups and Balls, Eggs, Hats, Handkerchiefs, &c. All from actual Experience. Edited by W. H. CREMER. 200 Illustrations.

Senior.—By Stream and Sea.

By W.SENIOR. Post 8vo,cl.limp, 2s.6d.

Seven Sagas (The) of Prehistoric Man.

By JAMES H. STODDART, Author of " The Village Life." Crown 8vo, cloth extra, 6s.

Shakespeare :

The First Folio Shakespeare.—MR. WILLIAM SHAKESPEARE'S Comedies, Histories, and Tragedies. Published according to the true Originall Copies. London, Printed by ISAAC IAGGARD and ED. BLOUNT. 1623.—A Reproduction of the extremely rare original, in reduced facsimile, by a photographic process—ensuring the strictest accuracy in every detail. Small 8vo, half-Roxburghe. 7s. 6d.

The Lansdowne Shakespeare. Beautifully printed in red and black, in small but very clear type. With engraved facsimile of DROESHOUT'S Portrait. Post 8vo, cloth extra, 7s. 6d.

Shakespeare for Children: Tales from Shakespeare. By CHARLES and MARY LAMB. With numerous Illustrations, coloured and plain, by J. MOYR SMITH. Cr. 4to, cl. gilt, 6s.

The Handbook of Shakespeare Music. Being an Account of 350 Pieces of Music, set to Words taken from the Plays and Poems of Shakespeare, the compositions ranging from the Elizabethan Age to the Present Time. By ALFRED ROFFE. 4to, half-Roxburghe, 7s.

SHAKESPEARE—continued.

A Study of Shakespeare. By ALGERNON CHARLES SWINBURNE. Crown 8vo, cloth extra, 8s.

Sheridan :—

Sheridan's Complete Works, with Life and Anecdotes. Including his Dramatic Writings, printed from the Original Editions, his Works in Prose and Poetry, Translations, Speeches, Jokes, Puns, &c. With a Collection of Sheridaniana. Crown 8vo, cloth extra, gilt, with 10 full-page Tinted Illustrations. 7s. 6d.

Sheridan's Comedies: The Rivals, and The School for Scandal. Edited, with an Introduction and Notes to each Play, and a Biographical Sketch of Sheridan, by BRANDER MATTHEWS. With Decorative Vignettes and 10 full-page Illusts. Demy 8vo, half-parchment, 12s. 6d.

Sidney's (Sir Philip) Complete

Poetical Works, including all those in "Arcadia." With Portrait, Memorial-Introduction, Notes, &c., by the Rev. A. B. GROSART, D.D. Three Vols., crown 8vo, cloth boards, 18s.

Signboards: Their History.

With Anecdotes of Famous Taverns and Remarkable Characters. By JACOB LARWOOD and JOHN CAMDEN HOTTEN. Crown 8vo, cloth extra, with 100 Illustrations, 7s. 6d.

Sims (George R.), Works by :

How the Poor Live. With 60 Illusts. by FRED. BARNARD. Large 4to, 1s.

Rogues and Vagabonds. Post 8vo, illust. boards, 2s ; cloth limp, 2s 6d.

The Ring o' Bells. Post 8vo, illust. bds., 2s. ; cloth, 2s. 6d.

Mary Jane's Memoirs. With a Photograph of Mary Jane. Post 8vo, illust. boards, 2s. ; cloth, 2s. 6d.

Sister Dora: A Biography. By

MARGARET LONSDALE. Popular Edition, Revised, with additional Chapter. a New Dedication and Preface, and Four Illustrations. Sq. 8vo, picture cover. 4d.; cloth, 6d.

Sketchley.—A Match in the

Dark. By ARTHUR SKETCHLEY. Post 8vo, illustrated boards, 2s.

Smith (J. Moyr), Works by :

The Prince of Argolis: A Story of the Old Greek Fairy Time. Small 8vo, cloth extra, with 130 Illusts., 3s. 6d.

Tales of Old Thule. With numerous Illustrations. Cr. 8vo, cloth gilt, 6s.

The Wooing of the Water Witch: A Northern Oddity. With numerous Illustrations. Small 8vo, cl. ex., 6s.

Slang Dictionary, The: Etymological, Historical, and Anecdotal. Crown 8vo, cloth extra, gilt, 6s. 6d.

Society in London. By A FOREIGN RESIDENT. New and Cheaper Edition, Revised, with an Additional Chapter on SOCIETY AMONG THE MIDDLE AND PROFESSIONAL CLASSES. Crown 8vo, 1s.; cloth, 1s. 6d.

Spalding.-Elizabethan Demonology: An Essay in Illustration of the Belief in the Existence of Devils, and the Powers possessed by Them. By T. A. SPALDING, LL.B. Cr. 8vo, cl. ex., 5s.

Spanish Legendary Tales. By Mrs. S. G. C. MIDDLEMORE, Author of "Round a Posada Fire." Crown 8vo, cloth extra, 6s.

Speight (T. W.), Novels by: The Mysteries of Heron Dyke. With a Frontispiece by M. ELLEN EDWARDS. Crown 8vo, cloth extra, 3s. 6d; post 8vo, illustrated bds., 2s. A Barren Title. Cr. 8vo, 1s.; cl., 1s.6d. Wife or No Wife? Cr. 8vo, picture cover, 1s.; cloth, 1s. 6d.

Spenser for Children. By M. H. TOWRY. With Illustrations by WALTER J. MORGAN. Crown 4to, with Coloured Illustrations, cloth gilt, 6s.

Staunton.—Laws and Practice of Chess; Together with an Analysis of the Openings, and a Treatise on End Games. By HOWARD STAUNTON. Edited by ROBERT B. WORMALD. New Edition, small cr. 8vo, cloth extra, 5s.

Stedman. — The Poets of America. With full Notes in Margin, and careful Analytical Index. By EDMUND CLARENCE STEDMAN, Author of "Victorian Poets." Cr. 8vo,cl.ex., 9s.

Stevenson (R.Louis), Works by: Travels with a Donkey in the Cevennes. Sixth Ed. Frontispiece by W. CRANE. Post 8vo, cl. limp, 2s. 6d. An Inland Voyage. With Front. by W. CRANE. Post 8vo, cl. lp., 2s. 6d. Familiar Studies of Men and Books. Second Edit. Crown 8vo, cl. ex., 6s. New Arabian Nights. Crown 8vo, cl. extra, 6s.; post 8vo, illust. bds., 2s. The Silverado Squatters. With Frontispiece. Cr. 8vo, cloth extra, 6s. Cheap Edition, post 8vo, picture cover, 1s.; cloth, 1s. 6d. Prince Otto: A Romance. Fourth Edition. Crown 8vo, cloth extra, 6s.; post 8vo, illustrated boards, 2s. The Merry Men, and other Tales and Fables. Cr. 8vo, cl. ex., 6s.

Sterndale.—The Afghan Knife: A Novel. By ROBERT ARMITAGE STERNDALE. Cr. 8vo, cloth extra, 3s. 6d.; post 8vo, illustrated boards, 2s.

St. John.—A Levantine Family. By BAYLE ST. JOHN. Post 8vo, illustrated boards, 2s.

Stoddard.—Summer Cruising in the South Seas. By CHARLES WARREN STODDARD. Illust. by WALLIS MACKAY. Crown 8vo, cl. extra. 3s. 6d.

Stories from Foreign Novelists. With Notices of their Lives and Writings. By HELEN and ALICE ZIMMERN. Frontispiece. Crown 8vo, cloth extra, 3s. 6d.; post 8vo, illust. bds., 2s.

St. Pierre.—Paul and Virginia, and The Indian Cottage. By BERNARDIN ST. PIERRE. Edited, with Life, by Rev. E. CLARKE. Post 8vo, cl. lp., 2s.

Strutt's Sports and Pastimes of the People of England; including the Rural and Domestic Recreations, May Games, Mummeries, Shows, &c., from the Earliest Period to the Present Time. With 140 Illustrations. Edited by WM. HONE. Cr. 8vo, cl. extra, 7s. 6d.

Suburban Homes (The) of London: A Residential Guide to Favourite London Localities, their Society, Celebrities, and Associations. With Notes on their Rental, Rates, and House Accommodation. With Map of Suburban London. Cr.8vo.cl.ex.,7s.6d.

Swift's Choice Works, in Prose and Verse. With Memoir, Portrait, and Facsimiles of the Maps in the Original Edition of "Gulliver's Travels." Cr. 8vo. cloth extra, 7s. 6d.

Swinburne (Algernon C.), Works by: Selections from the Poetical Works of Algernon Charles Swinburne. Fcap. 8vo, cloth extra, 8s. Atalanta in Calydon. Crown 8vo, 6s. Chastelard. A Tragedy. Cr. 8vo, 7s. Poems and Ballads FIRST SERIES. Fcap. 8vo, 9s. Cr. 8vo, same price. Poems and Ballads. SECOND SERIES. Fcap. 8vo, 9s. Cr. 8vo, same price. Notes on Poems and Reviews. 8vo,1s. Songs before Sunrise. Cr. 8vo, 1's.6d. Bothwell: A Tragedy. Cr.8vo,12s 6d. George Chapman: An Essay. Crown 8vo, 7s. Songs of Two Nations. Cr. 8vo, 6s. Essays and Studies. Crown 8vo, 12s. Erechtheus: A Tragedy. Cr.8vo, 6s. Note of an English Republican on the Muscovite Crusade. 8vo, 1s. Note on Charlotte Bronte.Cr.8vo,6s.

SWINBURNE'S (A. C.) WORKS, *continued—*
A Study of Shakespeare. Cr. 8vo, 8s.
Songs of the Springtides. Cr. 8vo, 6s.
Studies in Song. Crown 8vo, 7s.
Mary Stuart: A Tragedy. Cr. 8vo, 8s.
Tristram of Lyonesse, and other
Poems. Crown 8vo, 9s.
A Century of Roundels. Small 4to' 8s.
A Midsummer Holiday, and other
Poems. Crown 8vo, 7s.
Marino Faliero: A Tragedy. Cr.8vo,6s.
A Study of Victor Hugo. Cr. 8vo, 6s.
Miscellanies. Crown 8vo, 12s.

Symonds.—Wine, Women and
Song: Mediæval Latin Students'
Songs. Now first translated into Eng-
lish Verse, with Essay by J. ADDINGTON
SYMONDS. Small 8vo, parchment, 6s.

Syntax's (Dr.) Three Tours:
In Search of the Picturesque, in Search
of Consolation, and in Search of a
Wife. With the whole of ROWLAND-
SON'S droll page Illustrations in Colours
and a Life of the Author by J. C.
HOTTEN. Med. 8vo, cloth extra, 7s. 6d.

Taine's History of English
Literature. Translated by HENRY
VAN LAUN. Four Vols., small 8vo,
cloth boards, 30s.—POPULAR EDITION,
Two Vols., crown 8vo, cloth extra, 15s.

Taylor's (Bayard) Diversions
of the Echo Club: Burlesques of
Modern Writers. Post 8vo, cl. limp, 2s.

Taylor (Dr. J. E., F.L.S.), Works
by. Crown 8vo, cloth ex., 7s. 6d. each.
The Sagacity and Morality of
Plants: A Sketch of the Life and
Conduct of the Vegetable Kingdom.
Coloured Frontispiece and 100 Illust.
Our Common British Fossils, and
Where to Find Them: A Handbook
for Students. With 331 Illustrations.

Taylor's (Tom) Historical
Dramas: "Clancarty," "Jeanne
Darc," "'Twixt Axe and Crown." "The
Fool's Revenge," "Arkwright's Wife,"
"Anne Boleyn," "Plot and Passion."
One Vol., cr. 8vo, cloth extra, 7s. 6d.
*** The Plays may also be had sepa-
rately, at 1s. each.

Tennyson (Lord): A Biogra-
phical Sketch. By H. J. JENNINGS.
With a Photograph-Portrait. Crown
8vo, cloth extra, 6s.

Thackerayana: Notes and Anec-
dotes. Illustrated by Hundreds of
Sketches by WILLIAM MAKEPEACE
THACKERAY, depicting Humorous
Incidents in his School life, and
Favourite Characters in the books of
his every-day reading. With Coloured
Frontispiece. Cr. 8vo, cl. extra, 7s. 6d.

Thomas (Bertha), Novels by:
Crown 8vo, cloth extra, 3s. 6d. each;
post 8vo, illustrated boards, 2s. each.
Cressida. | Proud Maisie.
The Violin-Player.

Thomas (M.).—A Fight for Life:
A Novel. By W. MOY THOMAS. Post
8vo, illustrated boards, 2s.

Thomson's Seasons and Castle
of Indolence. With a Biographical
and Critical Introduction by ALLAN
CUNNINGHAM, and over 50 fine Illustrations on Steel and Wood. Crown 8vo,
cloth extra, gilt edges. 7s. 6d.

Thornbury (Walter), Works by
Haunted London. Edited by ED-
WARD WALFORD, M.A. With Illus-
trations by F. W. FAIRHOLT, F.S.A.
Crown 8vo, cloth extra. 7s. 6d.
The Life and Correspondence of
J. M. W. Turner. Founded upon
Letters and Papers furnished by his
Friends and fellow Academicians.
With numerous Illusts. in Colours,
facsimiled from Turner's Original
Drawings. Cr. 8vo, cl. extra, 7s. 6d.
Old Stories Re-told. Post 8vo, cloth
limp, 2s. 6d.
Tales for the Marines. Post 8vo,
illustrated boards, 2s.

Timbs (John), Works by:
Crown 8vo, cloth extra, 7s. 6d each.
The History of Clubs and Club Life
in London. With Anecdotes of its
Famous Coffee-houses, Hostelries,
and Taverns. With many Illusts.
English Eccentrics and Eccen-
t-icities: Stories of Wealth and
Fashion, Delusions, Impostures, and
Fanatic Missions, Strange Sights
and Sporting Scenes, Eccentric
Artists, Theatrical Folk, Men of
Letters, &c. With nearly 50 Illusts.

Trollope (Anthony), Novels by:
Crown 8vo, cloth extra, 3s. 6d. each;
post 8vo, illustrated boards, 2s. each.
The Way We Live Now.
Kept in the Dark.
Frau Frohmann. | Marion Fay.
Mr. Scarborough's Family.
The Land-Leaguers.
Post 8vo, illustrated boards, 2s. each.
The Golden Lion of Granpere.
John Caldigate. | American Senator

Trollope(Frances E.),Novels by
Crown 8vo, cloth extra, 3s. 6d. each;
post 8vo. illustrated boards, 2s. each.
Like Ships upon the Sea.
Mabel's Progress. | Anne Furness.

Trollope (T. A.).—Diamond Cut
Diamond, and other Stories. By
T. ADOLPHUS TROLLOPE. Post 8vo,
illustrated boards, 2s.

Trowbridge.—Farnell's Folly:
A Novel. By J. T. TROWBRIDGE. Post
8vo, illustrated boards, 2s.

Turgenieff. — Stories from
Foreign Novelists. By IVAN TURGE-
NIEFF, and others. Cr. 8vo, cloth extra,
3s. 6d.; post 8vo, illustrated boards, 2s.

Tytler (C. C. Fraser-). — Mistress Judith: A Novel. By C. C.
FRASER-TYTLER. Cr. 8vo, cloth extra,
3s. 6d.; post 8vo, illust. boards, 2s.

Tytler (Sarah), Novels by:
Crown 8vo, cloth extra, 3s. 6d. each;
post 8vo, illustrated boards, 2s. each.
What She Came Through.
The Bride's Pass.
Saint Mungo's City.
Beauty and the Beast.
Noblesse Oblige.
Lady Bell.

Crown 8vo, cloth extra, 3s. 6d. each.
Citoyenne Jacqueline.   Illustrated
by A. B. HOUGHTON.
The Huguenot Family. With Illusts.
Buried Diamonds.

Disappeared. With Six Illustrations
by P. MACNAB. Crown 8vo, cloth
extra, 6s.

Van Laun.—History of French
Literature. By H. VAN LAUN. Three
Vols., demy 8vo, cl. bds., 7s. 6d. each.

Villari.— A Double Bond: A
Story. By LINDA VILLARI. Fcap.
8vo, picture cover, 1s.

Walford (Edw., M.A.),Works by:
The County Families of the United
Kingdom. Containing Notices of
the Descent, Birth, Marriage, Educa-
tion, &c., of more than 12000, dis-
tinguished Heads of Families, their
Heirs Apparent or Presumptive, the
Offices they hold or have held, their
Town and Country Addresses, Clubs,
&c. Twenty-seventh Annual Edi-
tion, for 1887, cloth gilt, 50s.
The Shilling Peerage (1887). Con-
taining an Alphabetical List of the
House of Lords, Dates of Creation,
Lists of Scotch and Irish Peers,
Addresses, &c. 32mo, cloth, 1s.
Published annually.
The Shilling Baronetage (1887).
Containing an Alphabetical List of
the Baronets of the United Kingdom,
short Biographical Notices, Dates
of Creation, Addresses, &c. 32mo,
cloth, 1s.
The Shilling Knightage (1887). Con-
taining an Alphabetical List of the
Knights of the United Kingdom,
short Biographical Notices, Dates of
Creation, Addresses,&c. 32mo,cl.,1s.

WALFORD'S (EDW.) WORKS, continued—
The Shilling House of Commons
(1887). Containing a List of all the
Members of Parliament, their Tow n
and Country Addresses, &c. New
Edition, embodying the results of
the recent General Election. 32mo,
cloth, 1s. Published annually.
The Complete Peerage, Baronetage, Knightage, and House of
Commons (1887). In One Volume,
royal 32mo, cloth extra, gilt edges, 5s.

Haunted London.   By WALTER
THORNBURY. Edited by EDWARD
WALFORD, M.A. With Illustrations
by F. W. FAIRHOLT, F.S.A. Crown
8vo, cloth extra, 7s. 6d.

Walton and Cotton's Complete
Angler; or, The Contemplative Man's
Recreation; being a Discourse of
Rivers, Fishponds, Fish and Fishing,
written by IZAAK WALTON; and In-
structions how to Angle for a Trout or
Grayling in a clear Stream, by CHARLES
COTTON. With Original Memoirs and
Notes by Sir HARRIS NICOLAS, and
61 Copperplate Illustrations. Large
crown 8vo, cloth antique, 7s. 6d.

Walt Whitman, Poems by
Selected and edited, with an Introduction, by WILLIAM M. ROSSETTI. A
New Edition, with a Steel Plate Portrait. Crown 8vo, printed on hand-
made paper and bound in buckram, 6s.

Wanderer's Library, The:
Crown 8vo, cloth extra, 3s. 6d. each.
Wanderings in Patagonia; or, Life
among the Ostrich-Hunters. By
JULIUS BEERBOHM. Illustrated.
Camp Notes: Stories of Sport and
Adventure in Asia, Africa, and
America. By FREDERICK BOYLE.
Savage Life. By FREDERICK BOYLE.
Merrie England in the Olden Time.
By GEORGE DANIEL. With Illustra-
tions by ROBT. CRUIKSHANK.
Circus Life and Circus Celebrities.
By THOMAS FROST.
The Lives of the Conjurers. By
THOMAS FROST.
The Old Showmen and the Old
London Fairs. By THOMAS FROST.
Low-Life Deeps. An Account of the
Strange Fish to be found there. By
JAMES GREENWOOD.
The Wilds of London. By JAMES
GREENWOOD.
Tunis: The Land and the People.
By the Chevalier de HESSE-WAR-
TEGG. With 22 Illustrations.
The Life and Adventures of a Cheap
Jack. By One of the Fraternity.
Edited by CHARLES HINDLEY.
The World Behind the Scenes. By
PERCY FITZGERALD.

WANDERER'S LIBRARY, THE, *continued*—
Tavern Anecdotes and Sayings:
Including the Origin of Signs, and
Reminiscences connected with Ta-
verns, Coffee Houses, Clubs, &c.
By CHARLES HINDLEY. With Illusts.
The Genial Showman: Life and Ad-
ventures of Artemus Ward. By E. P.
HINGSTON. With a Frontispiece.
The Story of the London Parks.
By JACOB LARWOOD. With Illusts.
London Characters. By HENRY MAY-
HEW. Illustrated.
Seven Generations of Executioners:
Memoirs of the Sanson Family (1688
to 1847). Edited by HENRY SANSON.
Summer Cruising in the South
Seas. By C. WARREN STODDARD.
Illustrated by WALLIS MACKAY.

Warner.—A Roundabout Jour-
ney. By CHARLES DUDLEY WARNER,
Author of "My Summer in a Garden."
Crown 8vo, cloth extra. 6s.

Warrants, &c. :—
Warrant to Execute Charles I. An
exact Facsimile, with the Fifty-nine
Signatures, and corresponding Seals.
Carefully printed on paper to imitate
the Original, 22 in. by 14 in. Price 2s.
Warrant to Execute Mary Queen of
Scots. An exact Facsimile, including the Signature of Queen Elizabeth, and a Facsimile of the Great
Seal. Beautifully printed on paper
to imitate the Original MS. Price 2s.
Magna Charta. An exact Facsimile
of the Original Document in the
British Museum, printed on fine
plate paper, nearly 3 feet long by 2
feet wide. with the Arms and Seals
emblazoned in Gold and Colours. 5s.
The Roll of Battle Abbey; or, A List
of the Principal Warriors who came
over from Normandy with William
the Conqueror, and Settled in this
Country, A.D. 1066-7. With the
principal Arms emblazoned in Gold
and Colours. Price 5s.

Wayfarer, The: Journal of the
Society of Cyclists. Published Quar-
terly. Price 1s. Number I., for OCTO-
BER 1886, Number II., for JANUARY
1887, and Number III., for May, are
now ready.

Weather, How to Foretell the,
with the Pocket Spectroscope. By
F. W. CORY, M.R.C.S. Eng., F.R.Met.
Soc., &c. With 10 Illustrations. Crown
8vo, 1s. ; cloth, 1s. 6d.

Westropp.—Handbook of Pot-
tery and Porcelain; or, History of
those Arts from the Earliest Period.
By HODDER M. WESTROPP. With numerous Illustrations, and a List of
Marks. Crown 8vo, cloth limp, 4s. 6d.

Whistler's (Mr.) "Ten o'Clock."
Uniform with his "Whistler v. Ruskin:
Art and Art Critics." Cr.8vo,1s. [*Shortly.*

Williams (W. Mattieu, F.R.A.S.),
Works by :
Science Notes. See the GENTLEMAN'S
MAGAZINE. 1s. Monthly.
Science in Short Chapters. Crown
8vo, cloth extra, 7s. 6d.
A Simple Treatise on Heat. Crown
8vo, cloth limp, with Illusts., 2s. 6d.
The Chemistry of Cookery. Crown
8vo, cloth extra. 6s.

Wilson (Dr. Andrew, F.R.S.E.),
Works by:
Chapters on Evolution: A Popular
History of the Darwinian and
Allied Theories of Development.
Third Edition. Crown 8vo, cloth
extra, with 259 Illustrations, 7s. 6d.
Leaves from a Naturalist's Note-
book. Post 8vo, cloth limp, 2s. 6d.
Leisure-Time Studies, chiefly Bio-
logical. Third Edit., with New Pre-
face. Cr. 8vo. cl. ex., with Illusts., 6s.
Studies in Life and Sense. With
numerous Illustrations. Crown 8vo,
cloth extra, 6s.
Common Accidents, and How to
Treat them. By Dr. ANDREW WIL-
SON and others. With numerous Il-
lustrations. Crown 8vo, 1s. ; cloth
limp, 1s. 6d.

Winter (J. S.), Stories by :
Cavalry Life. Post 8vo, illust. bds., 2s.
Regimental Legends. Crown 8vo,
cloth extra, 3s. 6d. ; post 8vo, illustrated boards, 2s.

Women of the Day: A Biographical Dictionary of Notable Contemporaries. By FRANCES HAYS. Crown
8vo, cloth extra, 5s.

Wood.—Sabina: A Novel. By
Lady WOOD. Post 8vo, illust. bds., 2s.

Words, Facts, and Phrases :
A Dictionary of Curious, Quaint, and
Out-of-the-Way Matters. By ELIEZER
EDWARDS. New and cheaper issue,
cr. 8vo, cl. ex., 7s 6d. ; half-bound, 9s.

Wright (Thomas), Works by :
Crown 8vo, cloth extra. 7s. 6d each.
Caricature History of the Georges.
(The House of Hanover.) With 400
Pictures, Caricatures Squibs, Broad-
sides, Window Pictures, &c.
History of Caricature and of the
Grotesque in Art, Literature,
Sculpture, and Painting. Profusely
Illustrated by F.W. FAIRHOLT, F.S.A.

Yates (Edmund), Novels by :
Post 8vo, illustrated boards, 2s. each.
Castaway. | The Forlorn Hope
Land at Last.

NEW NOVELS.

NEW NOVEL by Author of "Mehalah."
Red Spider: A Romance. By Author "John Herring." Two Vols., cr. 8vo.

WILKIE COLLINS'S NEW STORIES.
Little Novels. By WILKIE COLLINS, Author of "The Woman in White." Three Vols., crown 8vo.

WALTER BESANT'S NEW NOVEL.
The World Went Very Well Then. Three Vols., crown 8vo.

CHRISTIE MURRAY'S NEW NOVEL
Old Blazer's Hero. By D. CHRISTIE MURRAY. Two Vols., crown 8vo, 12s. [*Shortly.*

JAMES PAYN'S NEW COLLECTION OF STORIES.
Glow-Worm Tales. By JAMES PAYN. Three Vols., crown 8vo.

NEW RUSSIAN REVOLUTIONARY NOVEL.
Radna; or, The Great Conspiracy of 1881. By the Princess OLGA. Crown 8vo, cloth extra, 6s.

SARAH TYTLER'S NEW NOVEL.
Disappeared: A Novel. By SARAH TYTLER, Author of "Saint Mungo's City," &c. With Six Illustrations by P. MACNAB. Cr. 8vo, cloth extra, 6s.

THE PICCADILLY NOVELS.

Popular Stories by the Best Authors. LIBRARY EDITIONS, many Illustrated, crown 8vo, cloth extra, 3s. 6d. each.

BY GRANT ALLEN.
Philistia.
In all Shades.

BY W. BESANT & JAMES RICE.
Ready-Money Mortiboy.
My Little Girl.
The Case of Mr. Lucraft.
This Son of Vulcan.
With Harp and Crown
The Golden Butterfly.
By Celia's Arbour.
The Monks of Thelema.
'Twas in Trafalgar's Bay.
The Seamy Side.
The Ten Years' Tenant.
The Chaplain of the Fleet.

BY WALTER BESANT.
All Sorts and Conditions of Men.
The Captains' Room.
All in a Garden Fair.
Dorothy Forster. | Uncle Jack.
Children of Gibeon.

BY ROBERT BUCHANAN.
Child of Nature.
God and the Man.
The Shadow of the Sword.
The Martyrdom of Madeline.
Love Me for Ever.
Annan Water. | The New Abelard.
Matt. | Foxglove Manor.
The Master of the Mine.

BY HALL CAINE.
The Shadow of a Crime.
A Son of Hagar.

BY MRS. H. LOVETT CAMERON.
Deceivers Ever. | Juliet's Guardian.

BY MORTIMER COLLINS.
Sweet Anne Page.|Transmigration.
From Midnight to Midnight.

MORTIMER & FRANCES COLLINS.
Blacksmith and Scholar.
The Village Comedy.
You Play me False.

BY WILKIE COLLINS.
Antonina.
Basil.
Hide and Seek.
The Dead Secret.
Queen of Hearts.
My Miscellanies.
Woman in White.
The Moonstone.
Man and Wife.
Poor Miss Finch.
Miss or Mrs. ?
New Magdalen.
The Frozen Deep.
The Law and the Lady.
The Two Destinies
Haunted Hotel.
The Fallen Leaves
Jezebel'sDaughter
The Black Robe.
Heart and Science
I Say No.

BY DUTTON COOK.
Paul Foster's Daughter.

BY WILLIAM CYPLES.
Hearts of Gold.

BY ALPHONSE DAUDET.
The Evangelist; or, Port Salvation.

BY JAMES DE MILLE.
A Castle in Spain.

BY J. LEITH DERWENT.
Our Lady of Tears.
Circe's Lovers.

BY M. BETHAM-EDWARDS.
Felicia. | Kitty.

BY MRS. ANNIE EDWARDES.
Archie Lovell.

BY PERCY FITZGERALD.
Fatal Zero.

BY R. E. FRANCILLON.
Queen Cophetua.
One by One.
A Real Queen.

Prefaced by Sir BARTLE FRERE.
Pandurang Hari.

BY EDWARD GARRETT.
The Capel Girls.

PICCADILLY NOVELS, *continued—*
BY CHARLES GIBBON.
Robin Gray. | For Luck of Gold.
What will the World Say?
In Honour Bound.
Queen of the Meadow.
The Flower of the Forest.
A Heart's Problem.
The Braes of Yarrow.
The Golden Shaft. | Of High Degree.
Fancy Free. | Loving a Dream.
A Hard Knot.

BY THOMAS HARDY.
Under the Greenwood Tree.

BY JULIAN HAWTHORNE.
Garth. | Ellice Quentin.
Sebastian Strome.
Prince Saroni's Wife.
Dust. | Fortune's Fool.
Beatrix Randolph.
Miss Cadogna.
Love—or a Name.

BY SIR A. HELPS.
Ivan de Biron.

BY MRS. CASHEL HOEY.
The Lover's Creed.

BY MRS. ALFRED HUNT.
Thornicroft's Model.
The Leaden Casket.
Self-Condemned.
That other Person.

BY JEAN INGELOW.
Fated to be Free.

BY HARRIETT JAY.
The Queen of Connaught.

BY R. ASHE KING.
A Drawn Game.
"The Wearing of the Green."

BY HENRY KINGSLEY.
Number Seventeen.

BY E. LYNN LINTON.
Patricia Kemball.
Atonement of Leam Dundas.
The World Well Lost.
Under which Lord?
With a Silken Thread.
The Rebel of the Family
"My Love!" | Ione.

BY HENRY W. LUCY.
Gideon Fleyce.

BY JUSTIN McCARTHY.
The Waterdale Neighbours.
My Enemy's Daughter.
A Fair Saxon.
Dear Lady Disdain.
Miss Misanthrope. | Donna Quixote
The Comet of a Season.
Maid of Athens.
Camiola.

BY MRS. MACDONELL
Quaker Cousins.

PICCADILLY NOVELS, *continued—*
BY FLORENCE MARRYAT.
Open! Sesame! | Written in Fire.

BY D. CHRISTIE MURRAY.
Life's Atonement. | Coals of Fire.
Joseph's Coat. | Val Strange.
A Model Father. | Hearts.
By the Gate of the Sea
The Way of the World.
A Bit of Human Nature.
First Person Singular.
Cynic Fortune.

BY MRS. OLIPHANT.
Whiteladies.

BY MARGARET A. PAUL.
Gentle and Simple.

BY JAMES PAYN.
Lost Sir Massing- | A Confidential
  berd. | Agent.
Best of Husbands | From Exile.
Halves. | A Grape from
Walter's Word. | Thorn.
What He Cost Her | For Cash Only.
Less Black than | Some Private
  We're Painted. | Views.
By Proxy | The   Canon's
High Spirits. | Ward
Under One Roof. | Talk of the Town.

BY E. C. PRICE.
Valentina. | The Foreigners.
Mrs. Lancaster's Rival.

BY CHARLES READE.
It Is Never Too Late to Mend.
Hard Cash.
Peg Woffington.
Christie Johnstone.
Griffith Gaunt. | Foul Play.
The Double Marriage.
Love Me Little, Love Me Long.
The Cloister and the Hearth.
The Course of True Love.
The Autobiography of a Thief.
Put Yourself in His Place.
A Terrible Temptation.
The Wandering Heir. | A Simpleton.
A Woman-Hater. | Readiana.
Singleheart and Doubleface.
The Jilt.
Good Stories of Men and other
  Animals.

BY MRS. J. H. RIDDELL.
Her Mother's Darling.
Prince of Wales's Garden-Party.
Weird Stories.

BY F. W. ROBINSON.
Women are Strange.
The Hands of Justice.

BY JOHN SAUNDERS.
Bound to the Wheel.
Guy Waterman.
Two Dreamers.
The Lion in the Path.

CHEAP POPULAR NOVELS, *continued*—
WILKIE COLLINS, *continued.*

Man and Wife.	Haunted Hotel.
Poor Miss Finch.	The Fallen Leaves.
Miss or Mrs.?	Jezebel's Daughter
New Magdalen.	The Black Robe.
The Frozen Deep.	Heart and Science
Law and the Lady.	"I Say No."
The Two Destinies'	The Evil Genius.

BY MORTIMER COLLINS.

Sweet Anne Page.	From Midnight to
Transmigration.	Midnight.
A Fight with Fortune.	

MORTIMER & FRANCES COLLINS.

Sweet and Twenty.	Frances.

Blacksmith and Scholar.
The Village Comedy.
You Play me False.

BY DUTTON COOK.

Leo.	Paul Foster's Daughter.

BY C. EGBERT CRADDOCK.
The Prophet of the Great Smoky Mountains.

BY WILLIAM CYPLES.
Hearts of Gold.

BY ALPHONSE DAUDET.
The Evangelist; or, Port Salvation.

BY JAMES DE MILLE.
A Castle in Spain.

BY J. LEITH DERWENT.

Our Lady of Tears.	Circe's Lovers.

BY CHARLES DICKENS.

Sketches by Boz.	Oliver Twist.
Pickwick Papers.	Nicholas Nickleby

BY MRS. ANNIE EDWARDES.

A Point of Honour.	Archie Lovell.

BY M. BETHAM-EDWARDS.

Felicia.	Kitty.

BY EDWARD EGGLESTON.
Roxy.

BY PERCY FITZGERALD.

Bella Donna.	Never Forgotten.

The Second Mrs. Tillotson.
Polly.
Seventy-five Brooke Street.
The Lady of Brantome.

BY ALBANY DE FONBLANQUE.
Filthy Lucre.

BY R. E. FRANCILLON.

Olympia.	Queen Cophetua.
One by One.	A Real Queen.

Prefaced by Sir H. BARTLE FRERE.
Pandurang Hari.

BY HAIN FRISWELL.
One of Two.

BY EDWARD GARRETT.
The Capel Girls.

CHEAP POPULAR NOVELS, *continued*—
BY CHARLES GIBBON.

Robin Gray.	The Flower of the
For Lack of Gold.	Forest.
What will the	A Heart's Problem
World Say?	Braes of Yarrow.
In Honour Bound.	The Golden Shaft.
In Love and War.	Of High Degree.
For the King.	Fancy Free.
In Pastures Green	Mead and Stream.
Queen of the Mea-	Loving a Dream,
dow.	A Hard Knot.

BY WILLIAM GILBERT.
Dr. Austin's Guests.
The Wizard of the Mountain.
James Duke.

BY JAMES GREENWOOD.
Dick Temple.

BY JOHN HABBERTON.
Brueton's Bayou.

BY ANDREW HALLIDAY.
Every-Day Papers.

BY LADY DUFFUS HARDY.
Paul Wynter's Sacrifice.

BY THOMAS HARDY.
Under the Greenwood Tree.

BY J. BERWICK HARWOOD.
The Tenth Earl.

BY JULIAN HAWTHORNE.

Garth.	Sebastian Stromo
Ellice Quentin.	Dust.
Prince Saroni's Wife.	
Fortune's Fool.	Beatrix Randolph.

BY SIR ARTHUR HELPS.
Ivan de Biron.

BY MRS. CASHEL HOEY.
The Lover's Creed.

BY TOM HOOD.
A Golden Heart.

BY MRS. GEORGE HOOPER.
The House of Raby.

BY TIGHE HOPKINS.
'Twixt Love and Duty.

BY MRS. ALFRED HUNT.
Thornicroft's Model.
The Leaden Casket.
Self-Condemned.

BY JEAN INGELOW.
Fated to be Free.

BY HARRIETT JAY.
The Dark Colleen.
The Queen of Connaught.

BY MARK KERSHAW.
Colonial Facts and Fictions.

BY R. ASHE KING.
A Drawn Game.
"The Wearing of the Green."

BY HENRY KINGSLEY.
Oakshott Castle.

BY E. LYNN LINTON.
Patricia Kemball.
The Atonement of Leam Dundas.

CHEAP POPULAR NOVELS, *continued—*
BY JAMES RUNCIMAN.
Skippers and Shellbacks.
Grace Balmaign's Sweetheart.
Schools and Scholars.
BY W. CLARK RUSSELL.
Round the Galley Fire.
On the Fo'k'sle Head.
In the Middle Watch.
BY BAYLE ST. JOHN.
A Levantine Family.
BY GEORGE AUGUSTUS SALA.
Gaslight and Daylight.
BY JOHN SAUNDERS.
Bound to the Wheel.
One Against the World.
Guy Waterman.
The Lion in the Path.
Two Dreamers.
BY KATHARINE SAUNDERS.
Joan Merryweather.
Margaret and Elizabeth.
The High Mills.
Heart Salvage. | Sebastian.
BY GEORGE R. SIMS.
Rogues and Vagabonds.
The Ring o' Bells.
Mary Jane's Memoirs.
BY ARTHUR SKETCHLEY.
A Match in the Dark.
BY T. W. SPEIGHT.
The Mysteries of Heron Dyke.
BY R. A. STERNDALE.
The Afghan Knife.
BY R. LOUIS STEVENSON.
New Arabian Nights.
Prince Otto.
BY BERTHA THOMAS.
Cressida. | Proud Maisie.
The Violin-Player.
BY W. MOY THOMAS.
A Fight for Life.
BY WALTER THORNBURY.
Tales for the Marines.
BY T. ADOLPHUS TROLLOPE.
Diamond Cut Diamond.
BY ANTHONY TROLLOPE.
The Way We Live Now.
The American Senator.
Frau Frohmann.
Marion Fay.
Kept in the Dark.
Mr. Scarborough's Family.
The Land-Leaguers.
The Golden Lion of Granpere.
John Caldigate.
By FRANCES ELEANOR TROLLOPE
Like Ships upon the Sea.
Anne Furness.
Mabel's Progress.
BY J. T. TROWBRIDGE.
Farnell's Folly.

CHEAP POPULAR NOVELS, *continued—*
BY IVAN TURGENIEFF, &c.
Stories from Foreign Novelists.
BY MARK TWAIN.
Tom Sawyer.
A Pleasure Trip on the Continent of Europe.
A Tramp Abroad.
The Stolen White Elephant.
Huckleberry Finn.
Life on the Mississippi.
BY C. C. FRASER-TYTLER.
Mistress Judith.
BY SARAH TYTLER.
What She Came Through.
The Bride's Pass.
Saint Mungo's City.
Beauty and the Beast.
BY J. S. WINTER.
Cavalry Life. | Regimental Legends.
BY LADY WOOD.
Sabina.
BY EDMUND YATES.
Castaway. | The Forlorn Hope.
Land at Last.
ANONYMOUS.
Paul Ferroll.
Why Paul Ferroll Killed his Wife.

POPULAR SHILLING BOOKS.
Jeff Briggs's Love Story. By BRET HARTE.
The Twins of Table Mountain. By BRET HARTE.
Mrs. Gainsborough's Diamonds. By JULIAN HAWTHORNE.
Kathleen Mavourneen. By Author of "That Lass o' Lowrie's."
Lindsay's Luck. By the Author of "That Lass o' Lowrie's."
Pretty Polly Pemberton. By the Author of "That Lass o' Lowrie's."
Trooping with Crows. By Mrs. PIRKIS.
The Professor's Wife. By LEONARD GRAHAM.
A Double Bond. By LINDA VILLARI.
Esther's Glove. By R. E. FRANCILLON.
The Garden that Paid the Rent. By TOM JERROLD.
Curly. By JOHN COLEMAN. Illustrated by J. C. DOLLMAN.
Beyond the Gates. By E. S. PHELPS.
An Old Maid's Paradise. By E. S. PHELPS.
Burglars in Paradise. By E. S. PHELPS.
Doom: An Atlantic Episode. By JUSTIN H. MACCARTHY, M.P.
Our Sensation Novel. Edited by JUSTIN H. MACCARTHY, M.P.
A Barren Title. By T. W. SPEIGHT.
Wife or No Wife? By T. W. SPEIGHT
The Silverado Squatters. By R. LOUIS STEVENSON.

J. OGDEN AND CO. LIMITED, PRINTERS, GREAT SAFFRON HILL, E.C.